Collected Poems

A. D. HOPE

Collected Poems

1930-1965

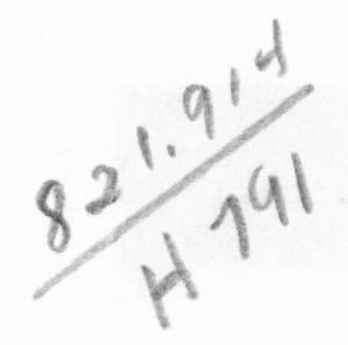

New York · THE VIKING PRESS

Published in 1966 by The Viking Press, Inc.
625 Madison Avenue, New York, N.Y. 10022

Distributed in Canada by The Macmillan Company of Canada Limited

Library of Congress catalog card number 66-14391
Printed in Australia

ACKNOWLEDGMENTS

The contents of this book are assembled, along with poems not previously published in book form, from *The Wandering Islands* (Sydney, Edwards and Shaw Ltd, 1955), *Poems* (London, Hamish Hamilton Ltd, 1960; New York, The Viking Press, 1962), and the volume *A. D. Hope* in the Australian Poets series (Sydney, Angus and Robertson Ltd, 1963). The author's thanks for permission to reprint are due to these publishers, and also to the following magazines in which some of the poems were first printed: the *Australian*, *Meanjin*, *Prospect*, *Quadrant*, *Southerly* and the *Texas Quarterly*.

PREFACE

I HAVE explained elsewhere in another preface to another book of poems that I do not think poets should write prefaces to their own works. Novelists may need this cosmetic aid since prose fiction is a comparatively amorphous and ambiguous art, but poetry should either speak for itself or not aspire to print at all. Having said this, I now proceed at the request of my publishers to write another preface for these *Collected Poems*. So much for consistency!

But if I do so it is to explain what the title really means. To me it suggests that I must be dead since I associate the words *Collected Poems* with the sort of publication normally entrusted to an eminent scholar after the author's demise, the sort of work which will contain a definitive text of all the known verse of the deceased, with dates and variant readings in the footnotes, and the whole thing decently interred between a bibliographical preface and an appendix of explanatory comments on the text. I am happy to say that this volume is nothing of the kind. Not only does it not contain, thank God, all the poems I have ever written, but it is also I hope merely a forerunner of many more to be written, now that I am approaching the age when I must give up the youthful folly of earning a living and put my energies to their proper work.

What this book represents is an anthology of those poems which I would still care to publish. I cannot remember an age at which I did not make up verses but my childish rhymes perished in an *auto-da-fé* at the age of fourteen when a friend persuaded me to burn them all and start again. Another fire, for which I was not responsible, later destroyed the evidence of prentice work up to the age of twenty-five. The present volume is a collection of poems written over the last thirty years. They are, roughly speaking, in the order in which they were written. I have left out a few facetious things, a long satire which is in process of revision, and a large number of manufacturer's seconds, fit only for the scrap-heap. If I am still blamed for preserving too much I can only say that there should be a difference between Selected Poems and Collected Poems. The former represents a writers own estimate of himself, the latter should, if it is an honest title, give the reader the evidence to make his own estimate.

A. D. HOPE

CONTENTS

With Chronological List of Poems

CONTENTS

CONTENTS

THE END OF A JOURNEY

There at the last, his arms embracing her,
She found herself, faith wasted, valour lost,
Raped by a stranger in her sullen bed;
And he, for all the bloody passion it cost
To have heard the sirens sing and yet have fled,
Thought the night tedious, coughed and shook his head,
An old man sleeping with his housekeeper.

But with the dawn he rose and stepped outside.
A farm-cart by the doorway dripped and stank,
Piled with the victims of his mighty bow.
Each with her broken neck, each with a blank,
Small, strangled face, the dead girls in a row
Swung as the cold airs moved them to and fro,
Full-breasted, delicate-waisted, heavy-thighed.

Setting his jaw, he turned and clambered down
A goat-track to the beach; the tide was full.
He stood and brooded on the breaking wave
Revolving many memories in his skull:
Calypso singing in her haunted cave,
The bed of Circe, Hector in his grave
And Priam butchered in his burning town.

Grimly he watched his enemy the sea
Rage round the petty kingdom he called home;
But now no trident threatened from the spray.
He prayed but knew Athene would not come.
The gods at last had left him, and the day
Darkened about him. Then from far away
And long ago, he seemed once more to be

Roped to a mast and through the breakers' roar
Sweet voices mocked him on his reeling deck:
"Son of Laertes, what delusive song
Turned your swift keel and brought you to this wreck,
In age and disenchantment to prolong
Stale years and chew the cud of ancient wrong,
A castaway upon so cruel a shore?"

THE DAMNATION OF BYRON

When the great hero, adding to the charms
Of genius and his scandals, left the light
Stamped with the irresistible trade of arms,
The Hell of Women received him as their right.

Through the Infernal Fields he makes his way
Playing again, but on a giant stage,
His own Don Juan; pursuing day by day
Childe Harold's last astonishing pilgrimage.

It is the landscape of erotic dreams:
The dim, brown plains, the country without air
Or tenderness of trees by hidden streams,
But cactus or euphorbia here and there

Thrusts up its monstrous phallus at the sky.
And moving against this silvered, lustrous green
Like a pink larva over the whole dry
Savannah of hell, the bodies of women are seen.

And at his coming all their beauties stir
Mysterious, like the freshening of a rose
As, the incomparable connoisseur,
Pale and serene across their world he goes,

Always there rises glowing in his path,
Superb and sensual, in the light that pours
A tarnished glory on the soil of death,
This leafless nakedness of tropic flowers;

The female body's impersonal charm, the curves
Of a young head poised on its gracious stalk.
The idiom of her gesture he observes,
That tender dislocation of her walk.

Held in his brain's deep lupanar they float,
The tapering trunk, the pure vase of the hips,
The breasts, the breasts to which the hands go out
Instinctive, the adoring finger-tips,

The thighs incurved, the skin misted with light,
The mouth repeating its own rich circumflex . . .
At first he moves and breathes in his delight
Drowned in the brute somnambulism of sex.

He is a kind of symbol of the male:
As a great bull, stiffly, deliberately
Crosses his paddock, lashing his brutal tail,
The sullen engine of fecundity,

So, in his first youth and his first desire,
His air of pride and the immortal bloom,
Once more he sets the feminine world on fire,
Passing in his romantic blaze of gloom.

Prodigious vigour flowers new in him:
Each morning nerves him with heroic lust.
His thoughts are women, he breathes, is clothed with them,
He sinks on something female in the dust.

He has them all, all the menagerie
Of race, the subtle stimulus of shapes:
Negresses in their first nubility
With the sad eyes and muzzles of young apes,

Vast Scandinavian divinities
Superbly modelled, for all their cowlike air,
The pale bread of their bellies' magnificent rise
From the blond triangle of pubic hair,

And slender girls with delicate golden shanks
And elongated skulls from lost Peru . . .
And sensual emphasis of the Spaniard's flanks,
And the callipygous haunches of the Jew. . . .

Dancers and whores, blue-stockings, countesses,
Types of La Fornarina and Caroline Lamb,
All the seductions of all mistresses,
The savage, the sentimental and the sham . . .

And yet he is alone. At first he feels
Nothing above the tumult of his blood,
While through his veins like the slow pox there steals
The deep significance of his solitude.

And from this feeling without haste or pause
Vengeance predestined sharpens, bit by bit;
As lust its anaesthesia withdraws
The force of his damnation grows from it.

Grows as the mind wakes, and inexorably
The critic, the thinker, the invincible
Intelligence at last detached and free
Wakes, and he knows . . . he knows he is in hell.

And there begins in him that horrible thing,
Clairvoyance, the cruel nightmare of escape:
He seeks companions: but they only bring
Wet kisses and voluptuous legs agape . . .

He longs for the companionship of men,
Their sexless friendliness. He cannot live
"Like the gods in Lucretius once again"
Nor ever in woman's wit and charm forgive

The taint of the pervading feminine
Yet always to this nausea he returns
From his own mind—the emptiness within
Of the professional lover. As he learns

How even his own society has become
A horror, a loneliness he cannot bear,
The last stage of Don Juan's martyrdom,
The last supreme resources of despair

Appear, and brutally lucid he descends
Simply to treat them as The Enemy.
His lust becomes revenge, his ardour lends
Insatiable pleasure to his insanity.

As he exhausts himself in the delights
Of torture, gourmandising in their pain,
Hate eats his features out: it seethes and bites
Like a slow acid. It destroys his brain.

Yet this resource betrays him, even this,
For like tormented demons, they adore
Their torment. They revere like savages
The god's ferocity with lascivious awe.

Until, neurotic, hounded by strange fears,
At last his journey changes to a flight.
Delirious, broken, fugitive, he hears
Marching and countermarching in the night,

The panic of vague terrors closing in:
Whichever way he turns he hears them come.
Far off immeasurable steps begin,
Far off the ominous mumble of a drum,

And from the bounds of that dim listening land
Approaches with her grave incessant tread
The Eternal Goddess in whose placid hand
Are all the happy and all the rebellious dead.

Before her now he stands and makes his prayer
For that oblivion of the Second Death . . .
When suddenly those majestic breasts all bare
Riding the tranquil motion of her breath

Reveal the body of her divinity:
The torso spread marmoreal, his eyes
Downwards uncover its mighty line and see
Darkness dividing those prodigious thighs.

There as he stares, slowly she smiles at him . . .
And the great hero, mad with the terrible
Madness of souls, turns fleeing, while the dim
Plains heave with the immense derision of Hell.

PYGMALION

I

Now woman, if you have it in you to live,
This is your living body's prerogative.
You could not by yourself deliberate
What only my impatience could create,
And I can do no more. This guess of mine,
All my invention, my superb design,
My courage, my challenge, my security—
I built you out of nothing: now build for me.
With your divine intelligence possess
My work; I did not spend myself for less.
I want your suffering: the intense and bare
Strain of your will. I want to see you dare
This difficult thing, to walk with agony on
The knives of my imagination, one
I scarcely know—when even in your hands'
Least moving something perfectly understands
All I created you to feel and be.
So I receive you, so you come to me.
And as to this complete accord we move
The imbecility of commencing love
Repulsed, and the grey nauseas of fear
The body of my redeemer enters here.
And in myself this man I have willed to know
Wakes at long last. Although I planned it so
I did not know I had so much to bring,
So much I could not give and dared not lend,
Into these hands my spirit I commend . . .
O take it, for it is a precious thing.

II

They have dared the improbable dream, they have made it theirs;
The nightmare house of shadows and wavering airs
Enlarged and curtained, stuffed the window tight
With a blank shutter of its outward night;
Proportioned so the vast and stately bed
Blessed with the pillar of darkness at the head;
Tied the four posts with unseen dying flowers.
—Over its tall, black cliff the music pours
Nightlong and plunges smoothly to the deep—
And touching with their naked breasts asleep
They lie and have forgotten what joy it is
That first impulsive charity of a kiss
—Deep flows the stream: they do not hear it pass.
They do not know if near them stirs what was
The once beloved gesture, familiar pain.
They cannot wake back to those selves again;
By any intellectual vision learn
What precious thing frets in the weeping urn
Of their content. And though the landscape still
Guards the assenting accent of their hill
They will not look to see if it be there
Arrested yet against voluptuous air.
They have walked on, away, and out of mind
Over the world's end—what they ached to find
Abandoned—the hollow mountain ate them up.
No use to shout far down the spiral cup
Of the void ear; these bodies have taken over.
Look here for love—you will not find the lover . . .
Only a moment, it may be, they toss,
Smile, and so touch the treasure of their loss.

III

So I perceive this last astonishment
In you: that even the indifferent
And things outlived and lost and left behind
Do not remain unchanged within the mind,
But have their own life still, and that you grow
Daily in me, whether I will or no.
Now even at night and lying long awake
Descending step by step the stairs that take
Me down the dark—the grey enormous stair—
I cannot summon you as once you were:
You come with a new movement; the surprise
Of unaccustomed hands, reluctant eyes,
Menstrual, remote.
                                        Unsummoned, you are still
There: a cancer ripening in the will,
Pushing its intricate trespass furtively
In the soft belly fibre. Now I see
The horror of Love, the sprouting cannibal plant
That it becomes—O God! What do you want?
What do you want? Do you know where you are?
This is my room, my mind. Get out of here!
Take your damned clothes, your two-sex thoughts, your laugh!
Back to the simper on the photograph
That was your smile, and is your smile no more.
I have gone into my silence, closed a door
Upon the comfort of its emptiness.
Why do you trouble it then? And should you guess
The magic syllables, I have made it bare.
What do you hope? Even though I am there,
Do you expect your body again with me
To utter in its guttural majesty
The accent of life? . . . or would you dare to build

A garden suburb of kindness where we piled
Our terrible sexual landscape, heap on heap
Of raging mountains? No more! I know too well
My need of loss, how easily we keep
The vision that once could make the heart rebel
Changed to a song that gives the children sleep.

STANDARDIZATION

When, darkly brooding on this Modern Age,
The journalist with his marketable woes
Fills up once more the inevitable page
Of fatuous, flatulent, Sunday-paper prose;

Whenever the green aesthete starts to whoop
With horror at the house not made with hands
And when from vacuum cleaners and tinned soup
Another pure theosophist demands

Rebirth in other, less industrial stars
Where huge towns thrust up in synthetic stone
And films and sleek miraculous motor cars
And celluloid and rubber are unknown;

When from his vegetable Sunday School
Emerges with the neatly maudlin phrase
Still one more Nature poet, to rant or drool
About the "Standardization of the Race";

I see, stooping among her orchard trees,
The old, sound Earth, gathering her windfalls in,
Broad in the hams and stiffening at the knees,
Pause, and I see her grave malicious grin.

For there is no manufacturer competes
With her in the mass production of shapes and things.
Over and over she gathers and repeats
The cast of a face, a million butterfly wings.

She does not tire of the pattern of a rose.
Her oldest tricks still catch us with surprise.
She cannot recall how long ago she chose
The streamlined hulls of fish, the snail's long eyes,

Love, which still pours into its ancient mould
The lashing seed that grows to a man again,
From whom by the same processes unfold
Unending generations of living men.

She has standardized his ultimate needs and pains.
Lost tribes in a lost language mutter in
His dreams: his science is tethered to their brains,
His guilt merely repeats Original Sin.

And beauty standing motionless before
Her mirror sees behind her, mile on mile,
A long queue in an unknown corridor,
Anonymous faces plastered with her smile.

THE EXPLORERS

Once he sees into the landscape of their minds,
All those nice young girls, so properly brought up
To be sensible and attract, the poet finds
Not a street in the suburbs, gossip at the tennis club,

But a primitive world of unnecessary hurt
And ignorance, where words like wild beasts wander.
They go, like savages, always on the alert
Placating shadows, foreboding thunder.

Enormous jungles full of eyes and fears
Mumble and gulp around them as they walk
Out after school—"Have a nice walk, dears,
Hustled through that huge succulent, twisting dark?"—

They prowl, the terrible man-eating words; stare;
Snuffle in the tangles. The path slides like a snake.
"It's worse if you hurry, dear. Don't look! There's nothing there
I tell you." "Can they climb trees too?" "Oh *don't,* Oh don't look
    back!"

Walking in a tight herd the odd safari comes
Wearing incongruous elegance of spring fashions,
"Is my face on right, dear?" Silk stockings harnessed to their bums
Buck on high heels. And squeezing under rubber foundations

Giggles the uneasy blood. Between the trees
Eyes on long stalks come swivelling. Something awful
Dabs at the ladies' handbags. "Clutch your virginities
Closer, closer, my dear. A girl can't be too careful."

In these steaming forests, rotting as they grow.
Stanley would have turned back: Livingstone never had such
    courage.
"It may come any minute now, you never know.
Look out for it. I think a girl should keep herself for marriage."

The miraculous clearing in the jungle, the end of the hunt
And O, the relief at last and O, how safe is
The little brick cottage, the ration of lawn in front
And a kiss at the gate and a pair of trousers walking daily to the
    office.

AUSTRALIA

A Nation of trees, drab green and desolate grey
In the field uniform of modern wars,
Darkens her hills, those endless, outstretched paws
Of Sphinx demolished or stone lion worn away.

They call her a young country, but they lie:
She is the last of lands, the emptiest,
A woman beyond her change of life, a breast
Still tender but within the womb is dry.

Without songs, architecture, history:
The emotions and superstitions of younger lands,
Her rivers of water drown among inland sands,
The river of her immense stupidity

Floods her monotonous tribes from Cairns to Perth.
In them at last the ultimate men arrive
Whose boast is not: "we live" but "we survive",
A type who will inhabit the dying earth.

And her five cities, like five teeming sores,
Each drains her: a vast parasite robber-state
Where second-hand Europeans pullulate
Timidly on the edge of alien shores.

Yet there are some like me turn gladly home
From the lush jungle of modern thought, to find
The Arabian desert of the human mind,
Hoping, if still from the deserts the prophets come,

Such savage and scarlet as no green hills dare
Springs in that waste, some spirit which escapes
The learned doubt, the chatter of cultured apes
Which is called civilization over there.

FLOWER POEM

Not these cut heads posed in a breathless room,
Their crisp flesh screaming while the cultured eye
Feeds grublike on the double martyrdom:
The insane virgins lusting as they die!
Connoisseurs breathe the rose's agony;
Between their legs the hairy flowers in bloom

Thrill at the amorous comparison.
As the professor snips the richest bud
For his lapel, his scalpel of reason
Lies on the tray; the class yawns for its food—
Only transfusion of a poem's blood
Can save them, bleeding from their civilization—

Not this cut flower but the entire plant
Achieves its miracle from soil and wind,
Rooted in dung, dirt, dead men's bones; the scent
And glory not in themselves an end; the end:
Fresh seeding in some other dirty mind,
The ache of its mysterious event

As its frail root fractures the subsoil, licks
At the damp stone in passing, drives its life
Deeper to split the ancient bedded rocks
And penetrates the cave beneath, it curls
In horror from that roof. There in its grief
The subterranean river roars, the troll's knife
Winks on his whetstone and the grinning girls
Sit spinning the bright fibre of their sex.

EASTER HYMN

Make no mistake; there will be no forgiveness;
No voice can harm you and no hand will save;
Fenced by the magic of deliberate darkness
You walk on the sharp edges of the wave;

Trouble with soul again the putrefaction
Where Lazarus three days rotten lies content.
Your human tears will be the seed of faction,
Murder the sequel to your sacrament.

The City of God is built like other cities:
Judas negotiates the loans you float;
You will meet Caiaphas upon committees;
You will be glad of Pilate's casting vote.

Your truest lovers still the foolish virgins,
Your heart will sicken at the marriage feasts
Knowing they watch you from the darkened gardens
Being polite to your official guests.

MASSACRE OF THE INNOCENTS

after Cornelis van Haarlem

The big sweet muscles of an athlete's dream
Pose for the sporting picture; Herod's guard
Opposes the selected Ladies' Team.
The game is Murder, played as a charade.

The white meat of the woman, prime and sleek,
Fends off the bull male from her squealing spawn;
The tenderloin, the buttock's creamy cheek,
Against the gladiator's marble brawn.

This is the classic painter's butcher shop;
—Choice cuts from the Antique—Triumphant Mars
Takes his revenge, the whistling falchions swoop
Round Venus as the type of all mammas.

The game is Nightmare: now, in the grotesque
Abortion of his love-dream, she displays
The pale, ripe carcass of the odalisque,
Now the brood-female in her mastoid grace.

The unruptured egg shrieks in her fallow womb.
Freckled with blood his knife-arm plunges straight
For the fat suckling's throat. He drives it home
Full loaded with his contraceptive hate.

THE BED

The doctor loves the patient,
The patient loves his bed;
A fine place to be born in,
The best place to be dead.

The doctor loves the patient
Because he means to die;
The patient loves the patient bed
That shares his agony.

The bed adores the doctor,
His cool and skilful touch
Soon brings another patient
Who loves her just as much.

GIVING IT UP

The amputated cigarette
Still nags. He can't forget
The lost volcanic limb
So much a part of him,
The smoking finger which
In crooked wreathes would sketch
Detachment's abstract rose,
His ritual of repose.

Maimed of this human part
The wounded gestures start.
Recoil with panic shock:
"Thank you—I do not smoke!"

And where the empty sleeve
Hangs, grows the make-believe:
"Thank God—no more a slave,
What will-power, too, I have!"

Trampling the hungry sense,
Forgets the lost pretence
That served his desperate need,
One habit by which freed
From bullying lusts and hurts,
Man smokes and mind asserts:
"I think and therefore am
And do not give a damn!"

THE RETURN FROM THE FREUDIAN ISLANDS

When they heard Sigmund the Saviour in these coasts
The islanders were very much impressed;
Abandoned the worship of their fathers' ghosts
And dedicated temples to their guest,

Shocked and delighted as the saint revealed
The unacknowledged body and made them see,
Suppressed by corsets, morbidly concealed
In cotton combinations, neck to knee,

How it bred night-sweats, the disease of shame,
Corns, fluxions, baldness and the sense of sin,
How clothes to the Analytic Eye became
Fantasies, furtive symbols of the skin.

At first the doctrine took them all by storm;
Urged to be stark, they peeled as they were told;
Forgetting their rags had also kept them warm,
For the island climate is often extremely cold.

And if the old, the wry, the ugly shared
Some natural reluctance to begin it,
Enthusiasts all, the young at once declared
Their Brave Nude World, that had such people in it.

Till some discovered that stripping to the buff
Only exposed the symbol of The Hide:
Its sinister pun unmasked, it must come off,
The saint must preach The Visible Inside!

The saint, though somewhat startled at this view,
Trapped by the logic of his gospel, spent
Some time in prayer, and in a week or two,
To demonstrate the new experiment,

Breastless and bald, with ribbed arms, lashless eyes,
In intricate bandages of human meat,
With delicate ripple and bulge of muscled thighs,
The first skinned girl walked primly down the street.

Though there were many to admire her charms:
The strappings and flexures of twig-like toes, the skeins
And twisted sensitive cables of her arms,
The pectoral fans, the netting of nerves and veins:

Yet those who followed her example found
One lack—till Sigmund undertook to prove
How much their late behaviour centred round
A common skin disease they had called love.

And for a time they thoroughly enjoyed
The brisk intolerance of the purified,
In sects and schisms before The Holy Freud
Self-torn—while lesser saints were deified.

Till Faith, which never can let well alone,
From heresy and counter-heresy
Prompted the saint to bare beneath the bone
The Ultimate Visceral Reality.

Long time he mused before The Sacred Id,
Long prayed, before he finally began
And, purged, impersonal, uninhibited,
Produced at last The Basic Freudian Man.

At the Fertility Festival that year
The skinned men blushed to see the skeleton,
A bone-cage filled with female guts appear
Tottering before them in the midday sun.

Its slats and levering rods they saw, the full
Cogged horseshoe grin of two and thirty teeth,
The frantic eyeballs swivelling in the skull,
The swagging human umbles underneath,

The soft wet mottled granite of the lung
Bulge and collapse, the liver worn askew
Jauntily quiver, the plump intestines hung
In glistening loops and bolsters in their view,

And clear through gut and bowel the mashy chyme
Churn downward; jelled in its transparent sheath
The scowling foetus tethered, and the time-
Bomb tumour set unguessed its budded death.

And while for them with mannequin grace she swayed
Her pelvis, Sigmund, so that none should miss
The beauty of the new world he had made,
Explained The Triumph of Analysis:

Pimples and cramps now shed with pelt and thews,
No dreams to fright, no visions to trouble them,
For, where the death-wish and self-knowledge fuse,
They had at last The Human L.C.M. . . .

Here the saint paused, looked modestly at the ground
And waited for their plaudits to begin.
And waited . . . There was nothing! A faint, dry sound
As first a poet buttoned on his skin.

HELDENSAGEN

Pop-eye my hero, Everyman my refuge,
Ahab within, mad master of my craft,
My instinct Noah, safest on his wet raft
And only bed-wrecked in the bibulous deluge.

My evening bus seeks out her north-west passage
And I my hero in the comic strip.
In every age the hero has taken ship
Away from the Newer Deal, the Nobler Message.

Commercial travellers' tales from a slick Munchausen;
Plastic millenniums of the technocrat;
The tribal psychologist pulling out of my hat
His portrait of Mansoul as a bottled abortion;

Admirals with power to organize my search
For Ithaca through this ten years monstrous dream;—
To all Messiahs the same reply, I am
Sinbad and on this Roc you build no church!

OBSERVATION CAR

To be put on the train and kissed and given my ticket,
Then the station slid backward, the shops and the neon lighting,
Reeling off in a drunken blur, with a whole pound note in my
 pocket
And the holiday packed with Perhaps. It used to be very exciting.

The present and past were enough. I did not mind having my back
To the engine. I sat like a spider and spun
Time backward out of my guts—or rather my eyes—and the track
Was a Now dwindling off to oblivion. I thought it was fun:

The telegraph poles slithered up in a sudden crescendo
As we sliced the hill and scattered its grazing sheep;
The days were a wheeling delirium that led without end to
Nights when we plunged into roaring tunnels of sleep.

But now I am tired of the train. I have learned that one tree
Is much like another, one hill the dead spit of the next
I have seen tailing off behind all the various types of country
Like a clock running down. I am bored and a little perplexed;

And weak with the effort of endless evacuation
Of the long monotonous Now, the repetitive, tidy
Officialdom of each siding, of each little station
Labelled Monday, Tuesday—and goodness! what happened to
 Friday?

And the maddening way the other passengers alter:
The schoolgirl who goes to the Ladies' comes back to her seat
A lollipop blonde who leads you on to assault her,
And you've just got her skirts round her waist and her pants round
 her feet

When you find yourself fumbling about the nightmare knees
Of a pink hippopotamus with a permanent wave
Who sends you for sandwiches and a couple of teas,
But by then she has whiskers, no teeth and one foot in the grave.

I have lost my faith that the ticket tells where we are going.
There are rumours the driver is mad—we are all being trucked
To the abattoirs somewhere—the signals are jammed and unknowing
We aim through the night full speed at a wrecked viaduct.

But I do not believe them. The future is rumour and drivel;
Only the past is assured. From the observation car
I stand looking back and watching the landscape shrivel,
Wondering where we are going and just where the hell we are,

Remembering how I planned to break the journey, to drive
My own car one day, to have choice in my hands and my foot upon
    power,
To see through the trumpet throat of vertiginous perspective
My urgent Now explode continually into flower,

To be the Eater of Time, a poet and not that sly
Anus of mind the historian. It was so simple and plain
To live by the sole, insatiable influx of the eye.
But something went wrong with the plan: I am still on the train.

MORNING COFFEE

Reading the menu at the morning service:
—Iced Venusberg perhaps, or buttered bum—
Orders the usual sex-ersatz, and, nervous,
Glances around—Will she or won't she come?

The congregation dissected into pews
Gulping their strip teas in the luminous cavern
Agape's sacramental berry stews;
The nickel-plated light and clatter of heaven

Receive him, temporary Tantalus
Into the Lookingglassland's firescape.
Suckled on Jungfraumilch his eyes discuss,
The werwolf twins, their mock Sabellian rape.

This is their time to reap the standing scorn,
Blonde Rumina's crop. Beneath her leafless tree
Ripe-rumped she lolls and clasps the plenteous horn.
Cool customers who defy his Trinity

Feel none the less, and thrill, ur-vater Fear
Caged in the son. For, though this ghost behave
Experienced daughters recognize King Leer:
Lot also had his daughters in a cave.

Full sail the proud three-decker sandwiches
With the eye-fumbled priestesses repass;
On their swan lake the enchanted ice-creams freeze,
The amorous fountain prickles in the glass

And at the introit of this mass emotion
She comes, she comes, a balanced pillar of blood,

Guides through the desert, divides the sterile ocean,
Brings sceptic Didymus his berserk food,

Sits deftly, folding elegant thighs, and takes
Her time. She skins her little leather hands,
Conscious that wavering towards her like tame snakes
The polyp eyes converge. . . . The prophet stands

Dreading the answer from her burning bush:
This unconsuming flame, the outlaw's blow,
Plague, exodus, Sinai, ruptured stones that gush,
God's telegram: Dare Now! Let this people go!

THE GATEWAY

Now the heart sings with all its thousand voices
To hear this city of cells, my body, sing.
The tree through the stiff clay at long last forces
Its thin strong roots and taps the secret spring.

And the sweet waters without intermission
Climb to the tips of its green tenement;
The breasts have borne the grace of their possession,
The lips have felt the pressure of content.

Here I come home: in this expected country
They know my name and speak it with delight.
I am the dream and you my gates of entry,
The means by which I waken into light.

THE WANDERING ISLANDS

You cannot build bridges between the wandering islands;
The Mind has no neighbours, and the unteachable heart
Announces its armistice time after time, but spends
Its love to draw them closer and closer apart.

They are not on the chart; they turn indifferent shoulders
On the island-hunters; they are not afraid
Of Cook or De Quiros, nor of the empire-builders;
By missionary bishops and the tourist trade

They are not annexed; they claim no fixed position;
They take no pride in a favoured latitude;
The committee of atolls inspires in them no devotion
And the earthquake belt no special attitude.

A refuge only for the shipwrecked sailor;
He sits on the shore and sullenly masturbates,
Dreaming of rescue, the pubs in the ports of call or
The big-hipped harlots at the dockyard gates.

But the wandering islands drift on their own business,
Incurious whether the whales swim round or under,
Investing no fear in ultimate forgiveness.
If they clap together, it is only casual thunder

And yet they are hurt—for the social polyps never
Girdle their bare shores with a moral reef;
When the icebergs grind them they know both beauty and terror;
They are not exempt from ordinary grief;

And the sudden ravages of love surprise
Them like acts of God—its irresistible function
They have never treated with convenient lies
As a part of geography or an institution.

An instant of fury, a bursting mountain of spray,
They rush together, their promontories lock,
An instant the castaway hails the castaway,
But the sounds perish in that earthquake shock.

And then, in the crash of ruined cliffs, the smother
And swirl of foam, the wandering islands part.
But all that one mind ever knows of another,
Or breaks the long isolation of the heart,

Was in that instant. The shipwrecked sailor senses
His own despair in a retreating face.
Around him he hears in the huge monotonous voices
Of wave and wind: "The Rescue will not take place."

MEDITATION MUSIC

"The iteration of these lines brings gold—"
Touching this knob brings magic from the air;
The Djinni can transport you anywhere.
Give us the red-hot rhythm: Poor Tom's acold.

Give him this day, O Lord, his daily dope,
Lest at his window into outer fear,
The backless cupboard, peeping with his ear
He sit too long, or at his hagioscope

The drug wears off and he sees clear enough
Behind the solemn voices and the choir
Of reassurance, behind the screen of higher
Purpose, the blind men play their Blind Man's Bluff.

Leave the tap running with the food of love
That's still the soldier's medicine for fear;
"If you don't listen, then it isn't there!"
The music says so, chuckling in its sleeve.

This comfort is laid on to every room;
Poor Tom is cleverer than his fathers were;
Our air is patterned like their wallpaper.
Incredible sentimental roses boom

To bait the wheedling voice of retail trade.
The sweet bribe oozes stickily in the ear.
Under the bed the vox-box conjuror
Plays burglars—there's no need to be afraid;

The genuine nightmare's paid to know its place.
This programme has been packed with every care.
You can't go wrong; our sales talk theatre
Pulls down the curtain on the rotting face.

Latter day miracles are in reverse:
The Flesh is now made Word for all to hear;
Seeking its god the starving voice of prayer
Creeps in the marrow of the Universe,

Subsidized by a wise capitalist
—Its Sunday programmes keep him on the air—
But from the Heaviside Layer, in static, there
Cracks the reply: "I, GOD, do not exist!"

Turn up the music, then, and let it pour!
"It stops you thinking of your troubles, dear!
I hear they're bombing London over there;
I hear they've just blown up the house next door."

The isle is full of noises. Stay inside!
Outside there's only unconditioned air.
But any hour you can tune in to where
The bed-time story advances like the tide.

LYING ON THE LAWN

Pinioned by gravity
Against earth's carcass, I
View the deep cavity
Of midnight sky:

Matter no matter then,
Against the skull
Feel, too, the mass of men
Exert their pull.

Each a weak freedom gives
To walk, to run—
Weak for the mind that drives
Clear of the sun.

Westward Canopus sinks;
The tree unhurt
Turns east, the plant that thinks
Tears at the dirt,

Feels its red sap of thought
On mansoil bleed—
And still the wounded root
Of will unfreed

By its own act of life
Chained to the ground.
Love itself twists a knife
Hard in that wound.

PHALLUS

This was the gods' god,
The leashed divinity,
Divine divining rod
And Me within the me.

By mindlight tower and tree
Its shadow on the ground
Throw, and in darkness she
Whose weapon is her wound

Fends off the knife, the sword,
The Tiger and the Snake;
It stalks the virgin's bed
And bites her wide awake.

Her Bab-el-Mandeb waits
Her Red Sea gate of tears:
The blood-sponge god dilates,
His rigid pomp appears;

Sets in the toothless mouth
A tongue of prophecy.
It speaks in naked Truth
Indifference for me,

My huge irrelevance
Thought, passion, will, I know
Mere words that serve to fence
His obelisk of woe;

Love, a romantic slime
That lubricates his way
Against the stream of Time.
And though I win the day

His garrisons deep down
Ignore my victory,
Abandon this doomed town,
Crawl through a sewer and flee.

A certain triumph, of course,
Bribes me with brief joy:
Stiffly my Wooden Horse
Receive into your Troy.

ASCENT INTO HELL

Little Henry, too, had a great notion of singing.

—HISTORY OF THE FAIRCHILD FAMILY

I, too, at the mid-point, in a well-lit wood
Of second-rate purpose and mediocre success,
Explore in dreams the never-never of childhood,
Groping in daylight for the key of darkness;

Revisit, among the morning archipelagoes,
Tasmania, my receding childish island;
Unchanged my prehistoric flora grows
Within me, marsupial territories extend:

There is the land-locked valley and the river,
The Western Tiers make distance an emotion,
The gum trees roar in the gale, the poplars shiver
At twilight, the church pines imitate an ocean.

There, in the clear night, still I listen, waking
To a crunch of sulky wheels on the distant road;
The marsh of stars reflects a starry croaking;
I hear in the pillow the sobbing of my blood

As the panic of unknown footsteps marching nearer,
Till the door opens, the inner world of panic
Nightmares that woke me to unawakening terror
Birthward resume their still inscrutable traffic.

Memory no more the backward, solid continent,
From island to island of despairing dream
I follow the dwindling soul in its ascent;
The bayonets and the pickelhauben gleam

Among the leaves, as, in the poplar tree,
They find him hiding. With an axe he stands
Above the German soldiers, hopelessly
Chopping the fingers from the climbing hands.

Or, in the well-known house, a secret door
Opens on empty rooms from which a stair
Leads down to a grey, dusty corridor,
Room after room, ominous, still and bare.

He cannot turn back, a lurking horror beckons
Round the next corner, beyond each further door.
Sweating with nameless anguish then he wakens;
Finds the familiar walls blank as before.

Chased by wild bulls, his legs stick fast with terror.
He reaches the fence at last—the fence falls flat.
Choking, he runs, the trees he climbs will totter.
Or the cruel horns, like telescopes, shoot out.

At his fourth year the waking life turns inward.
Here on his Easter Island the stone faces
Rear meaningless monuments of hate and dread.
Dreamlike within the dream real names and places

Survive. His mother comforts him with her body
Against the nightmare of the lions and tigers.
Again he is standing in his father's study
Lying about his lie, is whipped, and hears

His scream of outrage, valid to this day.
In bed, he fingers his stump of sex, invents
How he took off his clothes and ran away,
Slit up his belly with various instruments;

To brood on this was a deep abdominal joy
Still recognized as a feeling at the core
Of love—and the last genuine memory
Is singing "Jesus Loves Me"—then, no more!

Beyond is a lost country and in vain
I enter that mysterious territory.
Lit by faint hints of memory lies the plain
Where from its Null took shape this conscious I

Which backward scans the dark—But at my side
The unrecognized Other Voice speaks in my ear,
The voice of my fear, the voice of my unseen guide;
"Who are we, stranger? What are we doing here?"

And through the uncertain gloom, sudden I see
Beyond remembered time the imagined entry,
The enormous Birth-gate whispering, *"per me,*
per me si va tra la perduta gente."

CONQUISTADOR

I sing of the decline of Henry Clay
Who loved a white girl of uncommon size.
Although a small man in a little way,
He had in him some seed of enterprise.

Each day he caught the seven-thirty train
To work, watered his garden after tea,
Took an umbrella if it looked like rain
And was remarkably like you or me.

He had his hair cut once a fortnight, tried
Not to forget the birthday of his wife,
And might have lived unnoticed till he died
Had not ambition entered Henry's life.

He met her in the lounge of an hotel
—A most unusual place for him to go—
But there he was and there she was as well,
Sitting alone. He ordered beers for two.

She was so large a girl that when they came
He gave the waiter twice the usual tip.
She smiled without surprise, told him her name,
And as the name trembled on Henry's lip,

His parched soul, swelling like a desert root,
Broke out its delicate dream upon the air;
The mountains shook with earthquake under foot;
An angel seized him suddenly by the hair;

The sky was shrill with peril as he passed;
A hurricane crushed his senses with its din;
The wildfire crackled up his reeling mast;
The trumpet of a maelstrom sucked him in;

The desert shrivelled and burnt off his feet;
His bones and buttons an enormous snake
Vomited up; still in the shimmering heat
The pygmies showed him their forbidden lake

And then transfixed him with their poison darts;
He married six black virgins in a bunch,
Who, when they had drawn out his manly parts,
Stewed him and ate him lovingly for lunch.

Adventure opened wide its grisly jaws;
Henry looked in and knew the Hero's doom.
The huge white girl drank on without a pause
And, just at closing time, she asked him home.

The tram they took was full of Roaring Boys
Announcing the world's ruin and Judgment Day;
The sky blared with its grand orchestral voice
The Götterdämmerung of Henry Clay.

But in her quiet room they were alone.
There, towering over Henry by a head,
She stood and took her clothes off one by one,
And then she stretched herself upon the bed.

Her bulk of beauty, her stupendous grace
Challenged the lion heart in his puny dust.
Proudly his Moment looked him in the face:
He rose to meet it as a hero must;

Climbed the white mountain of unravished snow,
Planted his tiny flag upon the peak.
The smooth drifts, scarcely breathing, lay below.
She did not take the trouble to smile or speak.

And afterwards, it may have been in play,
The enormous girl rolled over and squashed him flat;
And, as she could not send him home that way,
Used him thereafter as a bedside mat.

Speaking at large, I will say this of her:
She did not spare expense to make him nice.
Tanned on both sides and neatly edged with fur,
The job would have been cheap at any price.

And when, in winter, getting out of bed,
Her large soft feet pressed warmly on the skin,
The two glass eyes would sparkle in his head,
The jaws extend their papier-mâché grin.

Good people, for the soul of Henry Clay
Offer your prayers, and view his destiny!
He was the Hero of our Time. He may
With any luck, one day, be you or me.

TO JULIA WALKING AWAY

Darwin's daughters have no tails,
Yet a reminiscent motion
Agitates the lovely frails
At the seat of amputation.

Charles called Eve and Adam lies
And denied the garden state,
Yet the gait of Paradise
Could not wholly liquidate.

Julia's coccyx never can,
Swerving in delicious schism
Now to the Descent of Man,
Now towards Fundamentalism.

Darwin, Paley, from the dust
Argue in her ambulation:
Was Eve genuine, or just
A gorilla on probation?

THE CHEEK

Here's a new Genesis; the year is One;
This bed and we a world, our lamp its sun.
Love to its single dark dimension bound
Rules its volcano kingdom underground:
The feet at their remote antipodes
Twine their smooth roots; at Capricorn the knees
Nuzzle together; intershafted lies
The amplitude of firm and polished thighs;

And, pulsing in the liquid centre's heat
The angry sledges of the future beat
Hard on the groaning anvil of our joy.
These labouring ministers to one end employ
Our acts, the loins' harsh mat, the straining hips,
The moonbeam belly quaking in eclipse;
The sunbeam belly on her tropic rests;
In their north hemisphere the dreaming breasts,
Masking the baffled thunder of the heart,
Flower with promise; over every part
In the grave beauty of their ritual dance
The delicate erotic hands advance.

Out of this tunnel of touch homunculus
Broods in his cave-brow unaware of us.
So stands the lost explorer unaware
Upon the crust of earthquake; stands to stare,
The chart's false witness idle in his hand,
At the long fallow curve of newfound land.
Close to your cheek this manikin the eye,
Ruminates in a giant revery,
Evokes from its pure amplitude profound
Illusions of interminable ground,
And in his tiny world creates again
The noble movement of the lonely plain.

Vast as the Pampas or the empty sweep
Of virgin earth in its millennial sleep,
Out to the melancholy bounds of sight
The golden downlands ripen to the light;
The delicate groundswell of its contours swerve
In one voluptuous, enchanted curve
To break at last in this still atmosphere
Against the fabulous mountain of the ear.

There in those hills, folded against the skies
The metaphysical cavern overlies
Your world of yesterday, and down its groove
The pulses of our dying music move;
Our laughter and the words we speak as breath
Drum with their atoms on the vault beneath
And wake the dream, and, by the dream unbound
Pass from the body into the soul of sound.

But the cave's watcher does not see them go,
Those trembling syllables with their golden bough;
For him the hills at the horizon wear
The illimitable and lucid trance of air,
The upland slopes are bland, the golden rain
Drenches the vast envergure of the plain;
And, lost in contemplation, he surveys
Mountains of new imagination raise
Their heads of storm. Cradled in space it looms
Cloud upon cloud in rising whorls and coombs,
A heavenly whirlwind, huge with darkness curled
And gulfs of thunder over all his world,
Where, ruling our last element of air,
There broods the terrible passion of your hair.

THE LINGAM AND THE YONI

The Lingam and the Yoni
Are walking hand in glove,
O are you listening, honey?
I hear my honey-love.

The He and She our movers
What is it they discuss?

Is it the talk of Lovers?
And do they speak of us?

I hear their high palaver—
O tell me what they say!
The talk goes on for ever
So deep in love are they;

So deep in thought, debating
The suburb and the street;
Time-payment calculating
Upon the bedroom suite.

But ours is long division
By love's arithmetic,
Until they make provision
To buy a box of brick,

A box that makes her prisoner,
That he must slave to win
To do the Lingam honour,
To keep the Yoni in.

The mortgage on tomorrow?
The haemorrhage of rent?
Against the heart they borrow
At five or six per cent.

The heart has bought fulfilment
Which yet their mouths defer
Until the last instalment
Upon the furniture.

No Lingam for her money
Can make up youth's arrears:
His layby on the Yoni
Will not be paid in years.

And they, who keep this tally,
They count what they destroy;
While, in its secret valley
Withers the herb of joy.

RAWHEAD AND BLOODY BONES

Rawhead and Bloody Bones
Cuts himself another slice;
Incest, Aquinas owns,
Is a form of avarice.

This Belly too commits,
By a strange and self abuse,
Chin-chopper's titbits,
Meat of his own mint, chews.

"Know thyself!" says Tongue's root-
Bulb in the bone sconce:
Belly loves its own fruit,
Sucks on three sins at once.

Soul and Body both do
Thus, until, a limit passed,
Gullet severed, right through—
Grisly cud falls at last.

Spare your poet pious groans!
Give the poet no advice!
Rawhead and Bloody Bones,
Cut yourself another slice!

X-RAY PHOTOGRAPH

Mapped by its panoply of shade
There is the skull I shall not see
—Dark hollow in its galaxy
From which the blazing eye must fade—

And, though I cannot see it plain,
Within those stellar spaces roll
The countless sparks and whorls of soul:
My constellation of the brain.

These bones are calm and beautiful;
The flesh, like water, strains and clears
To show the face my future wears
Drowned at the bottom of its pool.

Then I am full of rage and bliss,
For in our naked bed I feel,
Mate of your panting mouth as well,
The deathshead lean toward your kiss;

And I am mad to have you here,
Now, Now, the instant shield of lust,
Deep in your flesh my flesh to thrust
Against a more tremendous fear.

For in a last analysis
The mind has finer rays that show
The woof of atoms, and below
The mathematical abyss;

The solid bone dissolving just
As this dim pulp about the bone;
And whirling in its void alone
Yearns a fine interstitial dust.

The ray that melts away my skin
Pales at that sub-atomic wave:
This shows my image in the grave,
But that the emptiness within

By which I know our contacts are
Delusive as a point of light
That froths against my shores of sight
Sent out from the remotest star,

So spent, that great sun's fiery head
Is scarcely visible; a ray
So ancient that it brings today
Word from a world already dead.

DRAGON MUSIC

"No other man makes love like you," she said:
His blood escaped in panic from her wound;
Through the dear mouth a dragon panted flame,
It lit the ancient treasures in the mound,
It tore him in four pieces in the bed—
No other lover, she said, was quite the same!

She did not see them there, the four men all
Wound in her arms, sharing his startled eyes:
Cocksure the Great Seducer crowed his song;
The virile bristles rustled down his thighs;
The golden feathers sprouted from his tail;
His heart's bronze warders smacked their mighty gong.

But the Slave's heart in that tremendous din
Burst counting the incredible troops of lust;
Her Old Boys' Union, with beer and hearty jokes,
Held celebrations, invited him to join,
Published their names in alphabetical lists,
Danced round the bonfire of his burning sex.

The Observer smiling landed from his yacht,
Notebook in hand, rubbed noses with the chief.
"The native girl's magnificent physique
Makes her insatiable in love," he wrote.
The surf ran moaning on the jagged reef;
His camera gave the customary click.

Grasping a bright bough from the sacred wood,
The Lover explored her dark and tender dream.
Among the ghosts he breathed her words for breath,
And in his veins the words became his blood,
Till his heart, leaping in ecstasy from her stream,
Died on the bank, thrashing in silver death.

THREE ROMANCES

I

The curtain splits. I face the night
Alone in a great gush of light.
The darkness claps and coughs and cries
And twinkles with its thousand eyes.

The music sobs on the long drawn
Sad prelude of a single horn,
Till, with a crash, it takes the bar
That greets the entrance of the star.

I do not know my cue, the part
Forgotten that I learned by heart,
Only the naked act burns clear
And, in that instant, She is here.

As down the centre of the stage
She stalks in her voluptuous rage,
Light shrieks on her elastic skin,
Her navel widens to a grin.

And, left and right, magnificent,
Her scowling thighs about me bent,
Their fathom of strength and thunder join
To brace the warm spathe of the loin.

The flutes in all this blaze and heat
Their long smooth strokes repeat, repeat,
The violins swiftlier, sweetlier call,
And then the trumpet shatters all.

Down through a hundred raptures I
Slide weakly out of her and lie
Like a wet worm upon the boards,
And nobody at all applauds.

For, as the lights go out, there falls
Starlight among the roofless stalls;
This audience died long ago;
Their bones sit rocking at the show.

The dry weeds shake beside your chair;
Your jaw-bone drops to the parterre;
And, from the lustre, clear and full,
One crystal tinkles on your skull.

II

Here are the weaving branches
Of that resplendent eye,
The rivers' wandering trenches
Left when the rivers dry.

And through the blank of summer
Their parching channels spread;
The last pools steam and shimmer;
The reeds are brown and dead.

For you are both the season
That brimmed their banks with rain
And the blind, wasting passion
That dries them out again.

The eye, whose large horizons
Were quick with liquid sight,
Now circles in your prison's
Impenetrable light.

III

How can your eyelids cover
The monsters of your sleep?
Above those pits they hover
And plunge into the deep.

The night of horror falters
About your dreadful dream;
The dead men by their halters
Hang straight; the rivers scream;

Their waters writhe in anguish;
The trees weep helpless tears;
The rusting windmills languish
And groan with windy fears;

And from the hollow mountain
A voice of bestial dread
Wails like a golden fountain
And tells you I am dead.

O, it is true, my darling!
Sleep on and never see
What things come creeping, crawling,
Down here to lie with me.

THE MUSE

To James McAuley, January 1945

She is Arachne. Instinct spins the net
Of her ferocious purpose in the night.
On her bared nerves the dew shakes bright and wet;
The angry goddess still with light
Tortures the web; for there the spider hangs
In loveliness no wisdom could invent
And conscious of the poison in her fangs.

She is Ariadne by the shore
Watching a black sail vanish on the sea,
While he, whose steps beyond the dreadful door
Were guided, and again set free,
The loutish prince forgets the path he trod;
And she, though she remembers, will consent
Soon to be tumbled by the drunken god.

She is Penelope. Nightlong at the loom
She must unravel the promise in her heart,
Subdue the monthly protest of the womb;
And still she knows, for all her art,
While its one poor design grows out of date,
The gods, who have all time, too late relent
And when her triumph comes, it comes too late.

THE DINNER

Angels have dined with men, and when they do,
All that they touch and taste takes blessing too.
The world that lies within a night and day,
Ended with evening, all things pass away,
And, a new heaven and a new earth begun,
We meet as two, and touch and smile as one.
Then on my sleeve you lay your brilliant hand
And lead me to the lighted table land.
All things expect you: walls and ceiling swim
In mellower light; the chairs stand straight and trim;
The tables dressed with snow behold you come;
The mouth of every crystal glass is dumb;
The knives and forks in silver order shine
And grace descends upon the food and wine.

Delicate, young and cradled in delight,
You take your seat and bare your teeth to bite—
What is my courage then to suffer this
Miracle of your metamorphosis!
For in that instant I behold the jaws
Of the most terrible of carnivores
Tear at its prey; the ravening human packs
Pull down their terrified victim in its tracks;
The wit, the charm, the grace, the pride of life
Adore the bloody edges of a knife!
The nakedness I had my arms about
Was gorged with death—I see the cayman's snout
Snap the deer's nostrils as they touch the flood;
The tiger's hairy muzzle sweet with blood;
The condor, flapping from the rocky peak,
Light on the carrion, plunge his grisly beak
Into the rotting porridge; through the dark

Slides the lithe, cold torpedo of the shark.
The air, the jungle, the salt, cannibal sea
Hold no more ruthless beast of prey than she.
For her the ox falls snoring in his blood;
The lamb is butchered for her daily food;
Her exquisite mouth, that smiles and tastes the wine,
Has killed by proxy a whole herd of swine—

Her exquisite mouth! As men, when at the worst,
Envy past ills, a vision succeeds the first
For which how gladly would I take again
That vision of the bloody mouths of men!
Now from the ancient past are conjured crude
Terrors of the black cave and the blind wood:
There sits the giant at his monstrous board,
The giantess, massive as her shaggy lord,
Squats at the spit and bastes the sizzling meat,
Dresses the trencher, serves and takes her seat,
And, leaning on the plank her full, warm breasts,
Looks in his face and smiles. He takes and tests
His six-foot knife—the little ribs spring wide;
He cuts the liver steaming from its side.
Talking in deep, soft, grumbling undertones
They gnaw and crack and suck the marrowy bones.
The titbits and choice meats they pluck and press
Each on the other, with grave tenderness,
And touch and laugh; their strange, fierce features move
With the delight and confidence of love.
I watch their loves, I see their human feast
With the doomed comprehension of the beast;
I feel the sweat creep through my bristling hair;
Hollow with rage and fear, I crouch and stare,
And hear their great jaws strip and crush and chew,
And know the flesh they rend and tear is you.

THE HOUSE OF GOD

Morning service! parson preaches;
People all confess their sins;
God's domesticated creatures
Twine and rub against his shins;

Tails erect and whiskers pricking,
Sleeking down their Sunday fur,
Though demure, alive and kicking,
All in unison they purr:

Lord we praise Thee; hear us Master!
Feed and comfort, stroke and bless!
And not too severely cast a
Glance upon our trespasses:

"Yesterday we were not able
To resist that piece of fish
Left upon the kitchen table
While You went to fetch the dish;

"Twice this week a scrap with Rover;
Once, at least, we missed a rat;
And we *do* regret, Jehovah,
Having kittens in Your hat!

"Sexual noises in the garden,
Smelly patches in the hall—
Hear us, Lord, absolve and pardon;
We are human after all!"

Home at last from work in Heaven,
This is all the rest God gets;

E

Gladly for one day in seven
He relaxes with His pets.

Looking down He smiles and ponders,
Thinks of something extra nice:
From His beard, O Joy, O wonders!
Falls a shower of little mice.

THE DREAM

Unable to speak, exhausted by the search,
He stood and stared his love and unbelief
For the incredible luck that brought them there;
The clatter and fury of the endless march
Now stilled, the whisper of his inward grief
Dripped on and filled the cave of his despair.

"Be quick! You have so little time," she said;
"Listen! My terror stands breathing on the stair;
And soon you must go back into the storm.
Darling!" she said, and made her body bare
And drew him down beside her on the bed,
"See, you are cold; come to my heart, be warm!"

Unable to speak, he touched her with his hand,
Fingering the witnesses of cheek and breast.
The bloody anguish breeding in the bone
Told its long exile, told of all the lands
Where the unresting heart, seeking its rest,
Finds always that its language is unknown.

They knew in that fierce, shuddering first embrace,
Clearer than words, more desperate than a cry,
All that their spirits had borne and could not say:
Journeys that always led to the wrong place,
The maps whose promises turned out a lie,
The messages that always went astray.

There in each other's gaze they saw the vast
Deserts of sand where round them wheeled and swept
Voices of pleading or insane abuse;
A jungle of hands clutched at them as they passed
Breaking the fingers they could not unloose;
And eyes of malice watched them while they slept;

And golden bodies, counterfeiting love,
Won them with grace or pity—they woke to know
Mechanical, alien arms about them close,
The piston sliding in its greasy groove;
The masks of beauty fell aside, to show
An ulcer of pleasure eating away the nose,

The maggots writhing in a fly-blown eye—
There they lost hope, and the sane world forgot,
And nightmare grew at last to be their home.
Mysterious names were scrawled across the sky;
They tried to leave but found their passports not
In order, or the permit had not come;

And had set out at last alone, at night,
To be sent back: the frontier had been closed.
Clutching their parcels they were made to wait
For years in rooms blazing with too much light;
Were called for questioning or, while they dozed,
Wakened by blows and screaming at the gate.

Their names were shouted; they were led away.
The guards were friendly, but they did not know
The destination, or they would not tell;
In storm and terror and boredom, day by day
They struggled over passes deep with snow
Or plodded across deserts they knew too well.

Year after year the march went on: they grew
Accustomed to the noise, the dust, the chain,
The never being alone, the senseless haste
From nowhere to some end that no one knew.
They lay at night and heard the torrents of rain
Lashing the roofs, a fury of ruin and waste.

One day among the mountains, in the rough
Streets of a steep, unknown, unfriendly town,
Marching at dusk, the labouring columns met.
Their eyes held; they stood still; the chain dropped off;
They looked about them and they were alone;
She smiled and spoke his name; her eyes were wet.

Unable to speak, he touched her with his hand;
Unhurried and unafraid they moved away.
The doors stood wide; they climbed the silent stair.
There the room opened like their promised land.
Quiet as death he stood and watched the way
Her fingers moved as she let down her hair.

So close they lay; so cold, so fierce, so still
Their joy! Their dream so deep, so strong and full,
Folded them nearer and remade their world.
She felt her breasts against his breast, the thrill
Of his quick breath; he felt, at last, the dull
Beat of his blood, her arms about him curled;

And little by little she warmed him with her love;
The lineaments of grace, the gesture of peace,
Became their language, their enchanted speech,
Clothed her with courage and filled her body and drove
Away his guilt and gave his gift release;
And all their acts were answered, each to each.

She felt the frosty rigor that bound him turned
To ease—But the bright warmth she gave became
A fever of heat. In wonder and dismay
She felt him filled with fire; her flesh was burned
And from his mouth an unendurable flame
Scorched her, and she cried out and shrank away

And leapt up; for the bed was all alight—
Unable to speak, he rose and left her there;
Unable to meet her eyes that gazed with such
Anguish and horror, went out into the night,
Burning, burning, burning in her despair
And kindling hurt and ruin at his touch.

THE ELEGY

Variations on a theme of the Seventeenth Century

Madam, no more! The time has come to eat.
The spirit of man is nourished, too, with meat.
Those heroes and the warriors of old—
Feasting between their battles made them bold.
When Venus in the west hung out her lamp,
The rattling sons of Mars marched home to camp;

And while around the fires their wounds were dressed,
And tale was matched with tale, and jest with jest,
Flagons of wine and oxen roasted whole
Refreshed their bodies and restored the soul.

Come, leave the bed; put on your dress; efface
Awhile this dazzling armoury of grace!
Flushed and rejoicing from the well-fought fight
Now day lies panting in the arms of night;
The first dews tremble on the darkening field;
Put up your naked weapons, the bright shield
Of triumph glinting to the early stars;
Call our troops home with trumpets from their wars;
And, as wise generals, let them rest and dine
And celebrate our truce with meat and wine.
See, the meek table on our service waits;
The devil in crystal winks beside our plates;
These veterans of love's war we shall repay
And crown with feasts the glories of the day.

Think no disgrace, if now they play a part
Less worthy of the soldiers of the heart.
Though these we led were granted, even as we,
Their moment's draught of immortality,
We do but snatch our instant on the height
And in the valleys still live out the night.
Yet they surrender nothing which is theirs.
Nature is frugal in her ministers;
Each to some humbler office must return,
And so must we. Then grudge it not, but learn
In this the noble irony of kind:
These fierce, quick hands that rove and clasp must find
Other employment now with knife and fork;
Our mouths that groaned with joy, now eat and talk;

These chief commanders, too, without debate,
Sink to the lowliest service of the state.
Only our eyes observe no armistice;
Sparkling with love's perpetual surprise,
Their bright vedettes keep watch from hill to hill
And, when they meet, renew the combat still.
And yet to view you would I linger on:
This is the rarest moment, soonest gone.
While now the marching stars invest the sky
And the wide lands beneath surrendered lie,
Their streams and forests, parks and fields and farms,
Like this rich empire tranquil in my arms,
Seem lovelier in the last withdrawing light
And, as they vanish, most enchant the sight.
Still let me watch those countries as they fade
And all their lucid contours sink in shade;
The mounting thighs, the line of flank and breast,
Yet harbour a clear splendour from the west;
Though twilight draws into its shadowy reign
This breathing valley and that glimmering plain,
Still let my warrior heart with fresh delight
Rove and reflect: "Here, here began the fight;
Between those gentle hills I paused to rest,
And on this vale the kiss of triumph pressed;
There, full encircled by the frantic foe,
I rode between the lilies and the snow;
And, in this copse that parts the dark and shine,
Plundered the treasures of the hidden mine;
Down those long slopes in slow retreat I drew;
And here renewed the charge; and here, anew
Met stroke with stroke and touched, at the last breath,
The unimagined ecstasy of death."

Full darkness! Time enough the lamps were lit.

Let us to dinner, Madam; wine and wit
Must have their hour, even as love and war,
And what's to come revives what went before.
Come now, for see the Captain of my lust,
He had so stoutly fought and stiffly thrust,
Fallen, diminished on the field he lies;
Cover his face, he dreams in paradise.
We, while he sleeps, shall dine; and, when that's done,
Drink to his resurrection later on.

AN EPISTLE FROM HOLOFERNES

"Great Holofernes, Captain of the Host,
To Judith: Greeting! And, because his ghost
Neither forgets nor sleeps, peace to her heart!
He, being dead, would play a nobler part;
Yet, being a spirit unpacified, must seek
Vengeance. Take warning then; for souls that speak
Truth to the living, must be fed with blood.
Do not neglect his rites: give him that food
Without which ghosts are powerless to control
Malice which breeds by nature in the soul.
Take down the shining scimitar again;
Slay him with a cock, a kid to ease his pain.
For otherwise his talk is double talk,
And he must haunt you. Then, where'er you walk,
Hear his blood dripping from your bag of meat
And, at your table, sitting in your seat,
See the Great Captain's carcass; in your bed
Always upon your pillow grins the Head;
And bloodier whispers that infect the mind

Revenge in dreams the unacted deed of kind.
Think not the Jews nor the Jews' god shall save:
Charms are not sovereign beyond the grave,
And he who warns you, though he wish you well,
Has arms to take and hold you even in Hell."
Thus in a fable once I spoke to you;
Now other times require I speak it new.
How easy it would be if this were all,
Dear, then the house might totter: it should not fall;
Then, we should utter with our living breath
A healing language from the mouths of death;
In Judith you, in Holofernes I
Might know our legend. But, in days gone by,
This would have been a magic rod whose blow
Broke the parched rocks and made their waters flow.
We should have certainty to conjure with,
Acting the saving ritual of our myth;
The earthquake over, the air sweet and still,
Take courage against this sickness of the will;
For when in former times the myths were true,
For every trouble there was a thing to do:
He, who in faith assumed his Hero's part,
Performed a solemn cleansing of the heart:
The lustral waters, spilling from the bowl,
Poured on the guilty hands and purged the soul;
And sacred dances acted as a spell
To set a lid upon the Hideous Well.
Myths formed the rituals by which ancient men
Groped towards the dayspring and were born again.
Now, though the myths still serve us in our need,
From fear and from desire we are not freed;
Nor can the helpless torment in the breast
Act out its own damnation and have rest.
Yet myth has other uses: it confirms

The heart's conjectures and approves its terms
Against the servile speech of compromise,
Habit which blinds, custom which overlies
And masks us from ourselves—the myths define
Our figure and motion in the Great Design,
Cancel the accidents of name and place,
Set the fact naked against naked space,
And speak to us the truth of what we are.
As overhead the frame of star and star
Still sets rejoicing on the midnight air
Orion's girdle, Berenice's hair,
So when we take our legend for a guide
The firmament of vision opens wide.
Against the sweep of dark and silence lie
Our constellations spread upon the sky.
Plain is the language of those glorious ones;
The meteors flash through their glittering bones;
Freed from the sun of custom, they describe
What, by the daylight vision of the tribe,
We felt, unseeing. We in the mythic night
Know our own motion, burn with our own light,
Study high calm and shining, scorn the more
The beast that winks and snuffles at the door.

Yet the myths will not fit us ready made.
It is the meaning of the poet's trade
To re-create the fables and revive
In men the energies by which they live,
To reap the ancient harvests, plant again
And gather in the visionary grain,
And to transform the same unchanging seed
Into the gospel-bread on which they feed.
But they who trust the fables over much
Lose the real world, plain sight and common touch,

And, in their mythopoeic fetters bound,
Stand to be damned upon infernal ground,
Finding, no matter to what creed they look,
Half their salvation was not in the book.
Then books turn vampires and they drink our blood,
They who feed vampires join the vampire's brood
And, changed to hideous academic birds,
Eat living flesh and vomit it as words.
Our wills must re-imagine what they act
And in ourselves find what the fable lacked.
The myths indeed the Logos may impart,
But *verbum caro factum* is our part.
Thus, though our legend with its proving flame
Burns all to essence, shows in you the same
Temper of ancient virtue, force of will,
That saved the trembling people on the hill;
Though I myself in Holofernes know
Your bloody and greedy and insensate foe
And, at my feast, hear a relentless voice
Declare my grim dichotomy of choice:
Sound a retreat, or move to one event:
The headless carrion rolling in the tent;
Yet imaged new the fable is not plain:
Though Judith live and though the foe be slain,
Ours is a warfare of a different kind
Pitched in the unknown landscape of the mind,
Where both sides lose, yet both sides claim the day
And who besieges whom is hard to say;
Where each, by other foes encircled round,
Hears in the night far off the bubbling sound
Of the sweet springs that are to both denied,
And sees false watch-fires crown the mountain-side.
Where shall we turn? What issue can there be?
Through the waste woods we searched and found the Tree,

Sole of its kind, bowed with its precious fruit;
And lo, the great snake coiling round the root!
Was all our toil, our patience, then, for this?
Our prayers translated to a brutal hiss?
Our desperate hopes, the fears and dangers passed,
To end in death and terror at the last?
Reach me your hand; the darkness, gathering in,
Shrouds us—for now the mysteries begin:
The world we lost grows dim and yet on high
Figures of courage glitter in the sky;
And, though a desert compass us around,
Layers of water lie beneath that ground;
The fissure in the rock that sets them free
Feeds and refreshes our Forbidden Tree.
Already, though we do not feel it yet,
The unexpected miracle is complete;
Already, through the midnight hours, unseen
They rise and make these barren places green
Till the parched land in which we lost our way
Gives grace and power and meaning to the day,
Renews the heart, gives joy to every act
And turns the fables into living fact.
If in heroic couplets, then, I seem
To cut the ground from an heroic theme,
It is not that I mock at love, or you,
But, living two lives, know both of them are true.
There's a hard thing, and yet it must be done,
Which is: to see and live them both as one.
The daylight vision is stronger to compel,
But leaves us in the ignorance of hell;
And they, who live by starlight all the time,
Helpless and dangerous, blunder into crime;
And we must learn and live, as yet we may,
Vision that keeps the night and saves the day.

THE MARTYRDOM OF ST TERESA

There was a sudden croon of lilies
Drifting like music through the shop;
The bright knives flashed with heavenly malice,
The choppers lay in wait to chop;

And Jesus with his crown of briar
Worn like a little hat in *Vogue*
Picked up her soul of ruby fire
And popped it in his shopping bag.

She was so small a saint, a holy
Titbit upon the butcher's block—
Death chose the cuts with care and slowly
Put on his apron, eyed the clock

And sitting down serenely waited
Beside the plump brown carcass there,
Which kings had feared and the popes hated,
Which had known neither hate nor fear;

While through all Spain mysterious thunder
Woke cannibal longings in the blood,
Inviting man to put asunder
The flesh that had been joined with God.

The little nuns of her foundation
Arrived on foot, by mule or cart,
Each filled with meek determination
To have an elbow, or the heart.

Death with a smile expertly slices
A rib for one, for one the knee,

Cuts back a breast, cuts deeper, prises
Out the raw heart for all to see;

In Sister Philomena's basket
Safe for St Joseph's lies an arm;
The saw shrills on a bone, the brisket
Becomes a miracle-working charm;

At five to six Death drops his cleaver:
The sunset, as the crowd goes home,
Pours down on every true believer
The mystic blood of martyrdom.

THE PLEASURE OF PRINCES

What pleasures have great princes? These: to know
Themselves reputed mad with pride or power;
To speak few words—few words and short bring low
This ancient house, that city with flame devour;

To make old men, their father's enemies,
Drunk on the vintage of the former age;
To have great painters show their mistresses
Naked to the succeeding time; engage

The cunning of able, treacherous ministers
To serve, despite themselves, the cause they hate,
And leave a prosperous kingdom to their heirs
Nursed by the caterpillars of the state;

To keep their spies in good men's hearts; to read
The malice of the wise, and act betimes;
To hear the Grand Remonstrances of greed,
Led by the pure; cheat justice of her crimes;

To beget worthless sons and, being old,
By starlight climb the battlements, and while
The pacing sentry hugs himself for cold,
Keep vigil like a lover, muse and smile,

And think, to see from the grim castle steep
The midnight city below rejoice and shine:
"There my great demon grumbles in his sleep
And dreams of his destruction, and of mine."

INVOCATION

To the gods all things are fair and good and right, but men hold some things wrong and some right.

HERAKLEITOS. FR. 61

You near, you watchful, you invisible one
In whom all just desires arise and end,
Inscrutable presence, guide, deliverer, friend,
Whose will against my will, at need, is done!

In the great dark behind me I see well
Purpose, beyond my purpose, draw me here.
Towards what end? Now, in my fortieth year,
I look into the light and cannot tell.

Little by little a wisdom that I lacked
Grows in this heart, to see and know your sign;
But not the habit of courage that should be mine:
Damnation still hangs on that naked act

By which the few, the free, the chosen light
Our way, and deeply live and proudly move,
Renew the uncompromising choice of love,
Engender power and beauty on our night.

That breed is in my bones: in me again
The spirit elect works out its mighty plan—
Yes, but that birth is hard. In the grown man
Habit corrupts the will with terror or pain.

My passion, my gift, my vision can I betray?
Must for my pride the innocent be undone?
How shall I act? My dangerous days come on;
The lion and the dragon fill each way.

For, if I do the dragon's will, I see
Custom is served—and I am lost indeed.
But in the lion's burning eyes I read
Unjust, severe, divine Necessity

Declare her law. Unmoved upon her hill
She guards the eternal measures of the world;
But at the laws of men her lip is curled,
The frantic devotees of good and ill.

All perish in the Herakleitan fire;
But grace and mastery are in her hand
And she grants those, who learn and understand,
Vision that crowns the might of their desire.

Then, as the poets, who alone defend
That darkness out of which our light is won,
Strengthen my love—but flash no beam upon
The future; show the meaning, not the end!

Lest the mind, knowing too well the things to be,
Lose its blind courage and forget its part,
And no more trust its lightnings, nor the heart
Kindle and quicken at the mystery.

PYRAMIS OR THE HOUSE OF ASCENT

This is their image: the desert and the wild,
A lone man digging, a nation piling stones
Under the lash in fear, in sweat, in haste;
Image of those demonic minds who build
To outlast time, spend life to house old bones—
This pyramid rising squarely in the waste!

I think of the great work, its secret lost;
The solid, blind, invincible masonry
Still challenges the heart. Neglect and greed
Have left it void and ruin; sun and frost
Fret it away; yet, all foretold, I see
The builder answering: "Let the work proceed!"

I think of how the work was hurried on:
Those terrible souls, the Pharaohs, those great Kings
Taking, like genius, their prerogative
Of blood, mind, treasure: "Tomorrow I shall be gone;

If you lack slaves, make war! The measure of things
Is man, and I of men. By this you live."

No act of time limits the procreant will
And to subdue men seems a little thing,
Seeing that in another world than this
The gods themselves unwilling await him still
And must be overcome; for thus the King
Takes, for all men, his apotheosis.

I think of other pyramids, not in stone,
The great, incredible monuments of art,
And of their builders, men who put aside
Consideration, dared, and stood alone,
Strengthening those powers that fence the failing heart:
Intemperate will and incorruptible pride.

The man alone digging his bones a hole;
The pyramid in the waste—whose images?
Blake's tower of vision defying the black air;
Milton twice blind groping about his soul
For exit, and Swift raving mad in his—
The builders of the pyramid everywhere!

THE TROPHY

This the builder cannot guess,
Nor the lover's utmost skill:
In the instant of success
Suddenly the heart stands still;

Suddenly a shadow falls
On the builder's finished plan,
And the cry of love appals
All the energies of man.

What dire symbol of the heart
Comes, then, from its ancient tomb?
Image both of love and art,
See the Roman soldier come!

What great captain breaks his rest
All the annals cannot tell—
Stone lies blank upon his breast;
Bitter laurel shades him well—

What great captain's rigid will
Checked in flight his rabble host,
Roused them, drove them, cheered them still,
Though they knew the battle lost;

And, when the campaign was won
By the single force of pride,
Heard the ghost within him groan,
Fell upon his sword and died.

THE DEATH OF THE BIRD

For every bird there is this last migration:
Once more the cooling year kindles her heart;
With a warm passage to the summer station
Love pricks the course in lights across the chart.

Year after year a speck on the map, divided
By a whole hemisphere, summons her to come;
Season after season, sure and safely guided,
Going away she is also coming home.

And being home, memory becomes a passion
With which she feeds her brood and straws her nest,
Aware of ghosts that haunt the heart's possession
And exiled love mourning within the breast.

The sands are green with a mirage of valleys;
The palm-tree casts a shadow not its own;
Down the long architrave of temple or palace
Blows a cool air from moorland scarps of stone.

And day by day the whisper of love grows stronger;
That delicate voice, more urgent with despair,
Custom and fear constraining her no longer,
Drives her at last on the waste leagues of air.

A vanishing speck in those inane dominions,
Single and frail, uncertain of her place,
Alone in the bright host of her companions,
Lost in the blue unfriendliness of space,

She feels it close now, the appointed season:
The invisible thread is broken as she flies;
Suddenly, without warning, without reason,
The guiding spark of instinct winks and dies.

Try as she will, the trackless world delivers
No way, the wilderness of light no sign,
The immense and complex map of hills and rivers
Mocks her small wisdom with its vast design.

And darkness rises from the eastern valleys,
And the winds buffet her with their hungry breath,
And the great earth, with neither grief nor malice,
Receives the tiny burden of her death.

CIRCE

after the painting by Dosso Dossi

Behind her not the quivering of a leaf
Flutters the deep enchantment of the wood;
No ripple at her feet disturbs the well;
She sits among her lovers dazed with grief,
Bewildered by the charge of alien blood.
Herself transfigured by the hideous spell

She sits among her creatures motionless,
Sees the last human shadow of despair
Fade from the sad, inquisitive, animal eyes,
The naked body of the sorceress
Mocked by the light, sleek shapes of feather and hair.
And as on snout and beak and muzzle dies

The melancholy trace of human speech,
For the first time her heart is rich with words
And with her voice she disenchants the grove.
The lonely island and the sounding beach
Answer with barks and howls, the scream of birds,
Her uncontrollable, aching cry of love.

WILLIAM BUTLER YEATS

To have found at last that noble, candid speech
In which all things worth saying may be said,
Which, whether the mind asks, or the heart bids, to each
Affords its daily bread;

To have been afraid neither of lust nor hate,
To have shown the dance, and when the dancer ceased,
The bloody head of prophecy on a plate
Borne in at Herod's feast;

To have loved the bitter, lucid mind of Swift,
Bred passion against the times, made wisdom strong;
To have sweetened with your pride's instinctive gift
The brutal mouth of song;

To have shared with Blake uncompromising scorn
For art grown smug and clever, shown your age
The virgin leading home the unicorn
And loosed his sacred rage—

But more than all, when from my arms she went
That blessed my body all night, naked and near,
And all was done, and order and content
Closed the Platonic Year,

Was it *not* chance alone that made us look
Into the glass of the Great Memory
And know the eternal moments, in your book,
That we had grown to be?

CHORALE

Often had I found her fair;
Most when to my bed she came,
Naked as the moving air,
Slender, walking like a flame.
In that grace I sink and drown:
Opening like the liquid wave
To my touch she laid her down,
Drew me to her crystal cave.
  Love me ever, love me long—
  Was the burden of her song.

All divisions vanish there;
Now her eyes grow dark and still;
Now I feel the living air
With contending thunder fill;
Hear the shuddering cry begin,
Feel the heart leap in her breast,
And her moving loins within
Clasp their strong, rejoicing guest.
  Love me now, O now, O long!
  Is the burden of her song.

Now the wave recedes and dies;
Dancing fires descend the hill;
Blessed spirits from our eyes
Gaze in wonder and are still.
Yes our wondering spirits come
From their timeless anguish freed:
Yet within they hear the womb
Sighing for the wasted seed.
  Love may not delay too long—
  Is the burden of their song.

THE SLEEPER

Our birth is but a sleep and a forgetting . . .

When the night comes, I get
Into my coffin; set
The soul's brutal alarm;
Pull the green coverlet
Over my face; lie warm,
Deaf to the black storm.

Ah, but the truce is vain:
Then Chaos comes again;
The Mind's insatiate eye
Opens on its insane
Landscape of misery,
And will not let me die.

A gunshot tears the brain—
That one quick crash of pain
Pays for a lasting sleep.
Be finished with it then!
What argument can keep
You from that step?

The argument of fear,
A whisper that I hear
A voice that haunts my bed:
"The only sleep is here;
Suffer your nightmare; dread
The daylight of the dead."

THE JUDGEMENT

Last Friday when the sun had set
Under the stars the world was quiet.
I dreamed our Grand Assize was met
And a great judge was there to try it.

I dreamed the bitter choice was past
That kept our lives so long asunder;
And in my arms I held you fast
Until that summons broke in thunder.

It filled the world and shook the sky,
Crying our names through all creation,
And doomed our guilty hearts to die,
And after death proclaimed damnation;

A voice of warning and lament
For grace and mercy vainly shown us;
And naked from our bed we went,
The first fresh dews of sleep upon us.

And, as towards judgement, you and I
In the cool darkness walked together,
I felt the softness of your thigh
That brushed mine like a night-bird's feather.

I felt the hapless grief that rose,
And found your hand and drew you nearer.
"Dear heart," you said and held me close,
"I weep for joy and not for terror;

"For joy that in your arms I lay
At last, nor cared that all men knew it;
And Heaven cannot take away
That bliss, nor Hell itself undo it."

Then once again the voice of dread
Called out two names in solemn warning—
And in my solitary bed
I woke to find the cold day dawning

Remembering, in helpless woe,
That love our bitter choice had ended
The doom we spoke so long ago
That no damnation now could mend it.

LOT AND HIS DAUGHTERS

I

The ruddy fire-glow, like her sister's eyes,
Flickered on her bare breasts and licked along
The ripeness of her savage flanks; a tongue
Of darkness curled between her restless thighs.

Black as the Syrian night, on her young head
Clustered the tendrils of their ancient vine;
The cave gaped with its drunken mouth; the wine
Babbled, unceasing, from the old man's bed:

"I have two daughters . . . let them serve your need
. . . virgins . . . but these, my guests . . . you understand"—
She crept in and lay down. Her Promised Land
Lay waiting for the sower with his seed.

She felt him stir; she felt herself embraced;
The tough old arms bit hard on loin and breast;
The great beard smothered her. She was possessed.
A lioness roared abruptly in the waste.

But Lot's grim heart was far away. Beside
The Jordan stream, in other days, he stood
And kept the great beast, raging, from her brood,
And drove his javelin through her tawny hide.

II

The sun above the hills raged in the height.
Within Lot's cave, his vine-stock's living screen
Filtered the noon-day glare to a dim green
And hung the fat grapes bunched against the light.

The rascal patriarch, the bad old man,
Naked and rollicking on his heap of straw,
Scratching his hairy cods—one drunken paw
Spilled the red liquor from its silver can.

His beard, white as a blossoming branch, gaped wide;
Out flew a laugh: "By God, the wine is out!
More wine!"
    The cavern rumbled to his shout.
Brown fingers pushed the leafy screen aside.

And, padding broadly with their barefoot tread,
Calm-eyed, big-bellied, purposeful and slow,
Lot's delicate daughters, in the bloom and glow
Of their fulfilment stood beside his bed.

Crafty from fear, reckless with joy and greed,
The old man held them in his crapulous eye:
Mountains of promise bulging in his sky;
Ark of his race; God's covenant to his seed.

They stooped to take his cup, tilted and poured;
The must rose mantling to the glittering rim;
And, as the heart of Lot grew bold in him,
It boasted and exulted in the Lord.

"The one Just Man from Sodom saved alive!
Did not His finger point me to this cave?
Behold His hand once more stretched out to save!
For Jahweh too is just. My seed shall thrive.

"Shall not the Judge of all the earth do right?
Why did his angels take me by the hand?
My tribe shall yet be numbered with the sand
Upon the shore and with the stars of night.

"With me it shall be as with Abraham.
Dark are His ways, but sure and swift to bless—
How should my ewes breed in the wilderness?
And lo, the Lord himself provides a ram!"

But Lot's resourceful daughters, side by side,
Smiled back, inscrutable, patient and content;
Their slender bodies, ripe and eloquent,
Swayed like the standing corn at harvest-tide.

And, conscious of what trouble stirred below
His words and flickered in his shrewd old eyes,
They placed the cup that kept their father wise
In that best wisdom, which is not to know.

THE LAMP AND THE JAR

You are that vessel full of holy oil:
Wisdom, unstirring in its liquid sleep,
Hoarded and cool, lucid and golden green,
Fills the pure flanks of the containing stone;
Here darkness mellows what the sunlit soil
To purposes unknown, for ends unseen,
Produced, and labour of unnumbered men.
All the unthinking earth with fret or toil
Reared, ripened, buried in the earth again,
Here lives, and living, waits: this source alone
Distils those fruitful tears the Muses weep.

And I, the lamp before the sacred ark,
The root of fire, the burning flower of light,
Draw from your loins this inexhaustible joy.
There the perpetual miracle of grace
Recurs, as, from its agony, the flame
Feeds the blind heart of the adoring dark;
And there the figures of our mystery,
The shapes of terror and inhuman woe,
Emerge and prophesy; there with the mark
Of blood upon his breast and on his brow,
An unknown king, with my transfigured face,
Bends your immortal body to his delight.

SPORTSFIELD

Goddess of light, Renewer of the mind,
Now, as of old, Desire of gods and men,
Return to earth, shine, bless and bring again
The festivals of love, the rites of kind!

Since now no more in field or sacred grove
Do men perform them, naked, fervent, proud:
Packed in a plush arena now, the crowd
Sit chewing or gape to see the sports of love.

The Olympian game brings all together at last;
For Lonely Heart today may join the team,
Lover by proxy now enact his dream,
Ex-player once more live over all the past.

The amateurs who practise in parked cars
Gather to watch the smooth professional game.
What if real life is never quite the same—
An orchestra accompanies the stars.

An umpire watches for the least mistake,
The ambulance is there if they should fall;
These players only have to watch the ball,
Hero and heroine in the brilliant fake.

See the hot favourite who always wins
Lead out the Bedroom Harriers with trained ease;
The Golden Girls run on with twinkling knees;
The Love Team takes the field, the sport begins.

The sexual athlete takes her by the hand,
Crosses the line and scores the first embrace;

Fountains of youth and reservoirs of grace,
The schoolgirls cheer them from the Members' Stand.

See how they run! With what delicious airs
She leads him on! Now Villainy makes a pass,
Tackles her low and lays her on the grass;
Still chewing, the crowd lean forward in their chairs.

All will be well: the muscular child of light
Arriving just when she seems doomed to yield,
As Lust, disqualified, limps from the field,
Kisses away her tears and holds her tight.

Now in the final play their lips are met—
The grandstand holds its breath, the field grows dark,
The ball between the bed-posts finds the mark
To win the match, love all, love game and set!

The watchers all go wild, they leap and scream;
The flabby muscles that never learned to play,
Now tense, now drunk with make-believe, obey
The all-compelling, all-compensating dream:

Winner take all! all win where none take part,
All play at love where love is only play;
Who cares if, grace and violence drained away,
This debt is charged against the bankrupt heart?

Goddess of kind, whom twilight and the dawn
Bare to our eyes, if, as of old, you still
Keep holiday with men, descend and fill
The loins with light, with honey the curving horn.

THE BRIDES

Down the assembly line they roll and pass
Complete at last, a miracle of design;
Their chromium fenders, the unbreakable glass,
The fashionable curve, the air-flow line.

Grease to the elbows Mum and Dad enthuse,
Pocket their spanners and survey the bride;
Murmur: "A sweet job! All she needs is juice!
Built for a life-time—sleek as a fish. Inside

"He will find every comfort: the full set
Of gadgets; knobs that answer to the touch
For light or music; a place for his cigarette;
Room for his knees; a honey of a clutch."

Now slowly through the show-room's flattering glare
See her wheeled in to love, console, obey,
Shining and silent! Parson with a prayer
Blesses the number-plate, she rolls away

To write her numerals in his book of life;
And now, at last, stands on the open road,
Triumphant, perfect, every inch a wife,
While the corks pop, the flash-light bulbs explode.

Her heavenly bowser-boy assumes his seat;
She prints the soft dust with her brand-new treads,
Swings towards the future, purring with a sweet
Concatenation of the poppet heads.

IMPERIAL ADAM

Imperial Adam, naked in the dew,
Felt his brown flanks and found the rib was gone.
Puzzled he turned and saw where, two and two,
The mighty spoor of Jahweh marked the lawn.

Then he remembered through mysterious sleep
The surgeon fingers probing at the bone,
The voice so far away, so rich and deep:
"It is not good for him to live alone."

Turning once more he found Man's counterpart
In tender parody breathing at his side.
He knew her at first sight, he knew by heart
Her allegory of sense unsatisfied.

The pawpaw drooped its golden breasts above
Less generous than the honey of her flesh;
The innocent sunlight showed the place of love;
The dew on its dark hairs winked crisp and fresh.

This plump gourd severed from his virile root,
She promised on the turf of Paradise
Delicious pulp of the forbidden fruit;
Sly as the snake she loosed her sinuous thighs,

And waking, smiled up at him from the grass;
Her breasts rose softly and he heard her sigh—
From all the beasts whose pleasant task it was
In Eden to increase and multiply

Adam had learned the jolly deed of kind:
He took her in his arms and there and then,

Like the clean beasts, embracing from behind,
Began in joy to found the breed of men.

Then from the spurt of seed within her broke
Her terrible and triumphant female cry,
Split upward by the sexual lightning stroke.
It was the beasts now who stood watching by:

The gravid elephant, the calving hind,
The breeding bitch, the she-ape big with young
Were the first gentle midwives of mankind;
The teeming lioness rasped her with her tongue;

The proud vicuña nuzzled her as she slept
Lax on the grass; and Adam watching too
Saw how her dumb breasts at their ripening wept,
The great pod of her belly swelled and grew,

And saw its water break, and saw, in fear,
Its quaking muscles in the act of birth,
Between her legs a pigmy face appear,
And the first murderer lay upon the earth.

PASIPHAE

There stood the mimic cow; the young bull kept
Fast by the nose-ring, trampling in his pride,
Nuzzled her flanks and snuffed her naked side.
She was a queen: to have her will she crept

In that black box; and when her lover leapt
And fell thundering on his wooden bride,
When straight her fierce, frail body crouched inside
Felt the wet pizzle pierce and plunge, she wept.

She wept for terror, for triumph; she wept to know
Her love unable to embrace its bliss
So long imagined, waking and asleep.
But when within she felt the pulse, the blow,
The burst of copious seed, the burning kiss
Fill her with monstrous life, she did not weep.

TOAST FOR A GOLDEN AGE

Ebrius haec fecit terris, puto, monstra Prometheus:
Saturnalicio lusit et ipse luto.

MARTIAL

Here's to you, all of you, objects of fun or resentment,
Hail-fellow gentlemen, friends, wherever you are!
Sitting at ease with your arm round ten stone of contentment,
Or treating your favourite ulcer with gin at the bar;

Leading the story-book life of the fabulous biped,
The Male Cinderella, the fairy godmother's chum;
When Father Bear growled: "There is somebody lying in *my* bed!"
You laughed in his face or gave him a kick in the bum.

And here you are living happily ever after
And buying a round of drinks to prove that you are,
Or holding the blonde in the moonlight helpless with laughter
At your line of talk in the parked expensive car.

You were born with hair on your chest and a voice like thunder,
You said: Bang, Bang, Bang! and everyone fell down dead:
All of your life you found, and little wonder,
The girls kept climbing in and out of your bed;

All of your life it was you who were asked to the party;
When the ship went down, it was you were saved from the wreck;
You slept like a top, you were fit and cheerful and hearty
And most of your troubles were solved by writing a cheque.

Your trousers were pressed, your well-bred, civilized features
Appeared in the press and everyone knew that face—
And that is why the committee of living creatures
Toasts you tonight as type of the human race.

For tonight is an anniversary celebration
By all the beasts of modest intelligence
For the pensive ape who invented civilization
And lived on his wits at the rest of the world's expense.

Tonight we celebrate the triumphs of reason
And the rational animal's most remarkable feat:
The way he contrives, in season and out of season,
To solve the problem of getting too much to eat.

For the Earth, our mother, at last has found a master:
She was slow and kindly, she laughed and lay in the sun—
Time strapped to his wrist, he made the old girl work faster,
Stripping her naked and shouting to make her run.

He chopped the mantle of pines from her beautiful shoulders,
He ripped her breasts for his vines, her belly for corn;
And she smiled and grew green again and did as he told her,
And trebled the bounty of her plenteous horn.

Till the soil grew parched and thin, and the famine followed;
So he broke new ground—but he bred as the locust bred—
The acres he sowed by day were always swallowed
By the rivers he sowed at night in his double-bed.

He cracked his stockwhip: that characteristic gesture
Made dust of the plains and the hurricane bore it away.
A thousand years had gone to making the pasture
Which the wind or the flood destroyed in a single day.

And that is why, though we understand tonight you
Are otherwise engaged, and we do not mind,
Your fellow creatures had chosen to invite you
As a representative specimen of your kind:

Not one of the masters of the human spirit,
But the common denominator of the mass;
Not the giver of grace or wisdom all inherit,
But a middle-aged, middle-brow male of the middle-class.

We would not like you to think your friends are jealous;
Their turn may come; they have waited since time began.
But if man is the measure of all things, as you tell us,
All things from you may take the measure of man.

So we wait and watch you, and feel the planet grow colder,
The deserts get larger—it's no use making a fuss—
We wait for the day when Time, speaking over your shoulder,
Remarks that the dog-in-the-manger has missed the bus;

When the heir to the silver spoons and the winning tickets
Has a pain inside him and suddenly loses his hair;
And he gropes in his heart, in his hat, in his fourteen pockets,
But the ticket is missing—the ticket has never been there.

THE RETURN OF PERSEPHONE

Gliding through the still air, he made no sound;
Wing-shod and deft, dropped almost at her feet,
And searched the ghostly regiments and found
The living eyes, the tremor of breath, the beat
Of blood in all that bodiless underground.

She left her majesty; she loosed the zone
Of darkness and put by the rod of dread.
Standing, she turned her back upon the throne
Where, well she knew, the Ruler of the Dead,
Lord of her body and being, sat like stone;

Stared with his ravenous eyes to see her shake
The midnight drifting from her loosened hair,
The girl once more in all her actions wake,
The blush of colour in her cheeks appear
Lost with her flowers that day beside the lake.

The summer flowers scattering, the shout,
The black manes plunging down to the black pit—
Memory or dream? She stood awhile in doubt,
Then touched the Traveller God's brown arm and met
His cool, bright glance and heard his words ring out:

"Queen of the Dead and Mistress of the Year!"
—His voice was the ripe ripple of the corn;
The touch of dew, the rush of morning air—
"Remember now the world where you were born;
The month of your return at last is here."

And still she did not speak, but turned again
Looking for answer, for anger, for command:
The eyes of Dis were shut upon their pain;
Calm as his marble brow, the marble hand
Slept on his knee. Insuperable disdain

Foreknowing all bounds of passion, of power, of art,
Mastered but could not mask his deep despair.
Even as she turned with Hermes to depart,
Looking her last on her grim ravisher
For the first time she loved him from her heart.

PROMETHEUS UNBOUND

Still fettered, still unconquered, still in pain,
Bold in his hope and steadfast in his right,
The Friend of Man on the Caucasian height
Saw one vast flash to northward blast the plain.
As Hermes, swooping down, struck off the chain
And raised him, smiling, in that dazzling light,
"Does the old tyrant, then, repent his spite,"
He asked, "or has Zeus ceased at last to reign?"

"His wisdom is not mocked," the god replied,
"Nor alters nor repeals the great decree.
These are his words: 'Go, set the Titan free;
And let his torment be to wander wide
The ashes of mankind from sea to sea,
Judging that theft of fire from which they died.' "

THE AGE OF INNOCENCE
OR DARWIN MORALIZED

. . . and therefore you must not grudge to find the same soul in an Emperor, in a Post-horse, and in a Mushroom, since no unreadiness in the soul, but an indisposition in the organs works this. And therefore though this soul could not move when it was a Melon, yet it may remember and now tell me, at what lascivious banquet it was served. And though it could not speak when it was a spider, yet it can remember, and now tell me, who used it for poison to attain dignity.

JOHN DONNE

"That was the Eocene, the Golden Age;
On the vast plains of that lost continent"
—the Lecturer coughed and paused to turn a page—
"Swarmed the first men, hairy and innocent,
And browsed and bred and slept and were content,
Their only speech short cries of joy and rage.

"Observe this skull: they were, as you can see,
Small-brained and simple-hearted, largely thewed.
Recent research in archaeology
Has proved the males magnificently endued
With virile force, the females handsome, nude,
Generous and quite devoid of coquetry.

"A touch, a nod and Nature did the rest:
Their loins were fruitful and the world was wide.
If I may be allowed a simple jest,
They could not count, but how they multiplied!
The earth with prodigal hand their wants supplied;
We might suppose them, then, supremely blest.

"Alas, we would be wrong: the state of man
Has never known uncomplicated bliss.
Like other species since the world began,
Natural selection makes him what he is.
The great Darwinian hypothesis
Knows no exception to its general plan.

"Nature provides a process of control
On her own limitless fecundity;
Each kind evolves to its mysterious goal
Thanks to some ruthless natural enemy.
The fittest to survive, survive. We see
In this the explanation of the soul.

"In these primordial men, I should explain,
Two types of primitive soul distinguished two
Species, and each a pure Mendelian strain;
The evidence suggests that each bred true.
One type was white and dazzling to the view;
One a soft black—" the Lecturer paused again,

Took off his spectacles and gazed around,
Then, delicately polishing each glass,
Replaced them magisterially and frowned.
"The soul of modern man," he told the class,
"Occurs in various shades of *grey*. Alas,
The old pure strains today are rarely found.

"But let us contemplate the Eocene
As it would be if we could travel back:
Men in unnumbered millions rove the green
And flowery lap of earth. Some have the knack
To hunt and snare small prey: their souls are black.
(Doubtless, some melanism in the gene.)

"They showed more wit than the albino kind,
Whose habits, strictly vegetarian,
Prove them more brutish, while the blacks inclined
More to the brutal: but at best we can
Hardly allow them, placed by modern man,
More than a rudimentary sort of mind.

"Over the heads of this dumb, wandering horde,
Darkening the sky, filling the reach of space,
Clouds of voracious spirits wheeled and soared,
Following their natural prey, the human race:
Angels, descending with rich cries of grace,
Exulted in the bounty of the Lord;

"While swarms of demons flocking to the spot,
Swooped down, with hideous shrieks of rage and hate,
To seize and rend their victims as they squat
At meat, or tear them while they copulate.
Yet, delicate feeders these, no flesh they ate,
Sucked the sweet souls and left the rest to rot.

"That crude black taste, the demons' chief delight,
Is something that the angels all detest;
While the bland milky flavours of the white
Sicken a healthy demon at the best.
But none for the rare *greys* showed any zest,
Fruit of mischance or blunders of the night.

"It follows, gentlemen, you will observe"
—the Lecturer beamed around the class and winked—
"That, following an asymptotic curve,
Both the pure species soon became extinct.
The Chain of Cause, inexorably linked,
Laid bare by that great science which we serve,

"Thus demonstrates the Progress of the Soul.
Throwbacks to black or white, indeed, arise;
But Nature in ourselves attains her goal:
The triumph of Adaptive Compromise!
In the grey eye of Science alone it lies
To see life steadily and see it whole."

FAFNIR

Under the stars the great wise Worm lay dead;
But all that night the hero played his part,
Rejoiced the bride and had her maidenhead.
Having tasted for her pleasure Fafnir's heart,
She woke at day-break in the tumbled bed.

In their cool, twilight world the birds began:
She knew their speech; the doom of human kind,
Brimming its banks and babbling as it ran,
Poured through the startled channels of her mind.
In that dim light she watched the sleeping man;

Saw Brynhild waken in the ring of fire,
Saw him with Brynhild in the marriage-bed,
Saw Brynhild wandering crazed with her desire,
The quarrel by the river and Sigurd dead
And Brynhild stretched beside him on the pyre.

Watching the naked man, a wild and grim
And brutal passion kindled in her heart;
She felt no fear; she did not pity him;
But saw with joy his body torn apart,
With love, the blood spout fresh from throat and limb.

The birds talked on, the world grew bright again;
She felt her children born and perish; she knew
Beauty and terror that shape the fates of men;
Her spirit grew hard with wisdom, and withdrew
From memory, and became the dragon's den.

Fierce with desire she watched him wake and stir,
And moved to meet him as he threw her back
And crushed her with his arms and mounted her.
Then Sigurd gazing down saw in the black
Pits of her eyes the endless past recur;

Until once more he met the dragon's stare
Watching him from that dark hole in the ground;
Once more he shuddered as Fafnir left the lair,
And, from the black intestines of the mound,
Came pouring coil on coil into the air.

THE TWENTY-SECOND SONNET OF LOUISE LABÉ

O happy, fortunate, shining Sun, to see
Your friend and mistress always face to face;
And happy Moon: Endymion's embrace
Waits you as honey stored awaits the bee!

Mars beholds Venus, Mercury on the wing
Glides through each heaven, each land, with even pace;
And Jove looks down and views in many a place
The lustier times and trophies of his spring.

See how the harmony that reigns on high
Links with its force these bodies of the sky,
But had they not their loves, in toil and pain
They would break frame and order, and disperse
With random steps through a wrecked universe
Like me to search, and search, like me, in vain.

THE YOUNG GIRL AT THE BALL

While the young girl, with her full breasts and thighs
Eloquent through her clothes, moves as a tree
Bends and returns against the torrents of air,
The voice of my Demon falters, the babble dies
Around me; and, as the music ends, I see
Her smile and watch her walking back to her chair.

When I was young I should have found in her arms
My venture, my voyage, the talisman and the sign,
Had I straddled her beautiful flanks or gathered her breast in my
hand.
Each turn of the fabulous way would be quick with alarms
Where the dreadful crags thrust up through their forests of pine
And the dragons stirred in their dens as I rode through that land.

Had I been older, I should have entered her gate
As a traveller coming home to the cherished fire
Of a house where the heart goes in and out at its need;
I should have learned to move to her music, to wait
Through all the returning seasons of desire
For ripeness, and seen her belly abundant with my seed.

I have journeyed; I have come home; it is late in the year to depart.
She will not move to my arms or come to my bed.
She turns and smiles into other eyes than mine.
What is it, then, tears at my animal heart?
As I watched her dance, in every gesture I read
The challenge, the summons, the unmistakeable sign

Of the sensual miracle: Now, at last, I see
Those hidden presences and powers, aware
Of a promise kept, of mysteries revealed;
Just as the eye observes from the motions of the tree
All the invisible energies of the air
In the toss and recoil of boughs in an open field.

MEDITATION ON A BONE

A piece of bone, found at Trondhjem in 1901, with the following runic inscription (about A.D. 1050) cut on it:
I loved her as a maiden; I will not trouble Erlend's detestable wife; better she should be a widow.

Words scored upon a bone,
Scratched in despair or rage—
Nine hundred years have gone;
Now, in another age,
They burn with passion on
A scholar's tranquil page.

The scholar takes his pen
And turns the bone about,
And writes those words again.
Once more they seethe and shout,
And through a human brain
Undying hate rings out.

"I loved her when a maid;
I loathe and love the wife
That warms another's bed:
Let him beware his life!"
The scholar's hand is stayed;
His pen becomes a knife

To grave in living bone
The fierce archaic cry.
He sits and reads his own
Dull sum of misery.
A thousand years have flown
Before that ink is dry.

And, in a foreign tongue,
A man, who is not he,
Reads and his heart is wrung
This ancient grief to see,
And thinks: When I am dung,
What bone shall speak for me?

THE MEETING

Now she lies dead before his eyes,
Who cut the heart out of her breast,
Looses as if in love her thighs
And, in her solemn beauty dressed,
How stern the grace, how full the feast!

Now her red love, no more denied,
Streams all one way and laughs to know
It leaves its prison gaping wide,
As, in her life it longed to go
And warm him with its moving tide.

Now the rich river of her hair
Flows to his feet and starts to rise,
And coils and whispers towards the bare
Pulse in the throat, and winds to tear
The eyeballs from his hollow eyes.

Now flesh with flesh, at last they meet,
Stiff in his agony he stands;
And feels how, savage, true and sweet,
Still clenched within his cruel hands,
The murdered heart begins to beat.

THE KINGS

The lion in deserts royally takes his prey;
Gaunt crags cast back the hunting eagle's scream.
The King of Parasites, delicate, white and blind,
Ruling his world of fable even as they,
Dreams out his greedy and imperious dream
Immortal in the bellies of mankind.

In a rich bath of pre-digested soup,
Warm in the pulsing bowel, safely shut
From the bright ambient horror of sun and air,
His slender segments ripening loop by loop,
Broods the voluptuous monarch of the gut,
The Tapeworm, the prodigious Solitaire.

Alone among the royal beasts of prey
He takes no partner, no imperial mate
Seeks his embrace and bears his clamorous brood;
Within himself, in soft and passionate play,
Two sexes in their vigour celebrate
The raptures of helminthine solitude.

From the barbed crown that hooks him to his host,
The limbless ribbon, fecund, flat and wet,
Sways as the stream's delicious juices move;
And, as the ripe joints rupture and are lost,
Quivers in the prolonged, delirious jet
And spasm of unremitting acts of love.

And Nature no less prodigal in birth
In savage profusion spreads his royal sway:
Herds are his nurseries till the mouths of men,

At public feasts, or the domestic hearth,
Or by the hands of children at their play,
Transmit his line to human flesh again.

The former times, as emblems of an age,
Graved the gier-eagle's pride, the lion's great heart,
Leviathan sporting in the perilous sea;
Pictured on History's or the Muse's page,
All knew the King, the Hero, set apart
To stand up stiff against calamity,

Breed courage amid a broken nation's groans,
Cherish the will in men about to die,
To chasten with just rule a barbarous tribe
And guard, at last, the earth that kept his bones.
And still the Muse, who does not flatter or lie,
Finds for our age a symbol to describe

The secret life of Technocratic Man,
Abject desire, base fear that shape his law,
His idols of the cave, the mart, the stye—
No lion at bay for a beleaguered clan,
No eagle with the serpent in his claw,
Nor dragon soter with his searing eye,

But the great, greedy, parasitic worm,
Sucking the life of nations from within,
Blind and degenerate, snug in excrement.
"Behold your dream!" she says. "View here the form
And mirror of Time, the Shape you trusted in
While your world crumbled and my heavens were rent."

TOTENTANZ: THE COQUETTE

Past Midnight! Silent in her charming room,
Nobly proportioned, feminine, richly plain,
One elegant femur balanced across its twin,
Sits her lank guest in the deep armchair's gloom,
The dandy's pose, one hand upon his cane,
A bald skull and a melancholy grin.

Outside a car stops purring at the kerb,
Swift footsteps mount the stair; the door flies wide;
She sweeps in, brilliant as a breaking wave;
The shimmer and swirl of skirts, and the superb
Gesture with which she lays her cloak aside—
The Watcher, sitting silent as the grave,

Thinks of some youthful Antony, in all
The panoply of battle, at the hour
Of victory disarming in the camp.
So in her silks, still sparkling from the ball,
Still breathless in the ecstasy of power,
She balances unseeing, turns up her lamp,

Unpins her torrent of hair, unclasps a jewel,
Moving to music still. The marvellous dress
Slides down; the dazzling gestures gleam and glance
While her tall glass reflects them, as a pool
Mirrors some creature of the wilderness
Rapt in its solitary ritual dance;

Some nubile sorceress at the noon of night,
Flitting by savage tarn or sacred well,
Rapt in the magic invocation of love,

Herself enchanted by that animal rite,
Herself the source and vigour of the spell
That leads an unknown lover to her grove.

Now naked to her glass, alive, alone,
In scrutiny or question see her stand
Aware at last of her mysterious guest,
The hollow stare, the rigid mask of bone.
Under her arm the lattice of a hand
Clips cold on the ripe triumph of her breast.

Stiffly she stands, considering awhile
The challenge of the male, the frank embrace.
Then, on one shuddering, voluptuous breath,
Leans back to her gaunt lover with a smile,
Half turning, with her plenitude of grace,
In sensuous surrender to her death.

THE TOMB OF PENTHESILEA

The Hero's tomb is gone;
Yet here beside,
A solitary stone
Speaks for the Hero's bride.
Trace, Traveller, with the tried
And dusty staff
Her epitaph:

"Stranger, here rusts the bright
Bare weapon won,
That day he faced in fight
The brutish horde alone,
And took from an unknown
Adversary
The wound, and me.

"The man who masters men,
Knows but his star.
Love must complete him then;
He learns from sword and scar
The purpose of his war,
And with firm tread
Tramps on the dead.

"In pride he drew his breath
Who mastered me:
So glorious the sheath,
That jewelled panoply,
How splendid then must be
The soul, the thin
True blade within!

"It was my pride to lie
And lightly press
Against a marching thigh;
To have his hand embrace
My armature of grace;
To watch, to keep
His helpless sleep;

"To flash in the loud war
On flesh; to feel
The bitter life-blood pour
Raging along the steel;
To know, and to conceal
My gift to know
His final foe;

"To triumph then in fate—
The great hour come,
The blade spoke out elate;
The hidden wound was dumb.
He knew, as death struck home,
In that, in this
Lay the sword's bliss."

PERSONS FROM PORLOCK

On awaking he appeared to himself to have a distinct recollection of the whole, and taking his pen, ink and paper, instantly and eagerly wrote down the lines that are here preserved. At this moment he was unfortunately called out by a person on business from Portlock. . . .

PREFATORY NOTE TO *Kubla Khan*

It was unfortunate: Poor S.T.C.!
Once in his life, once only among men,
Once in the process of Eternity,
It happened, and it will not happen again:
His dream unbidden took shape as poetry,
And waking, he recalled it, and his pen

Set down the magic lines—then came the dread
Summons from Porlock and the vision fled.

Fortunate Coleridge! He at least began.
Porlock was tardy, almost missed its cue;
Something at least was saved of *Kubla Khan,*
And Porlock's agent, give the man his due,
Paid him that single visit in the span
Of a long life of three score years and two.
The Ancient Mariner, it is fair to mention,
Escaped the Person's sinister attention.

The Swan of Porlock is a kind of duck;
It quacks and has a large, absurd behind—
Yes, on the whole, the poet was in luck.
Think of his fate had Porlock been less kind;
The paps of Porlock might have given him suck;
Teachers from Porlock organized his mind,
And Porlock's Muse inspired the vapid strain
Of: "Porlock, Loveliest Village of the Plain!"

And had his baffled genius stood the test,
With that one vision which is death to hide
Burning for utterance in the poet's breast,
Porlock might still be trusted to provide
Neighbours from Porlock, culled from Porlock's best,
The sweetest girl in Porlock for his bride,
In due course to surround him with some young
Persons from Porlock, always giving tongue.

Eight hours a day of honest Porlock toil,
And Porlock parties—useless to refuse—
The ritual gardening of Porlock soil,
Would leave him time still for a spare-time Muse—

And when with conscience murdered, wits aboil,
He shook the dust of Porlock from his shoes,
Some would be apt to blame him, some to scoff,
But others kindly come to see him off.

Porlock was gone: the marvellous dream was there.
"In Xanadu . . ."—He knew the words by rote,
Had but to set them down.
                    To his despair
He found a man from Porlock wore his coat,
And thought his thoughts; and, stolid in his chair,
A person fresh from Porlock sat and wrote:
"Amid this tumult Kubla heard from far
Voices of Porlock babbling round the bar."

SOLEDADES OF THE SUN AND THE MOON

For P. K. Page

Now the year walks among the signs of heaven,
Swinging her large hips, smiling in all her motions,
Crosses with dancing steps the Milky Valley.
Round her the primal energies rejoice;
All the twelve metaphysical creatures and the seven
Swift spheres adore her vigour; the five oceans
  Look up and hear her voice
Ring through the ebony vault, where Ara Celi
Flames, and the choiring stars at their devotions
  With pure and jubilant noise
Praise and proclaim four seasons in her belly.

Four glittering worms, they sleep curled up inside her,
The unborn children of our isolation.
Solstice or song, in swift pursuit forever
We grieve in separate festivals of light.
What winged stallion, what immortal rider
Forks those wild flanks? What milk of generation
  Fills at a thrust the bright
Throat of the womb? By what supreme endeavour
Do the chaste Muses still take inspiration
  And tune the strings aright
By the god's bow that twangs to slay and sever?

Aimer of pestilence, Lucifer of healing,
Destroyer of the piping faun, Apollo!
Join these divided hearts. In single chorus
The raving sybil and the lucid seer
Find words to the one music, each revealing
Light in the other's dark, dark in that shining, hollow
  Galactic hemisphere
Which spins the changeless images before us.
Sign after sign, the constellations follow,
  Mirrored across the year
Where Scorpio views her house of death in Taurus.

Where the Wise Archer hangs his glittering quiver
Each son of Leda greets a heavenly brother.
As country or sex or song or birth conspire
The hemispheres set their crystal walls between.
Narcissus in air, Narcissus in the river
Drown in an alien element, or smother
  The lives towards which they lean.
Yet, through the burning circles of desire,
Immortal spirits behold, each in the other:

His pillar of flame serene,
She, the unknown somnambulist of her fire.

Cradles of earth receive the salamander
But once at most in any generation;
Once in an age a desert tribe surprises
The solitary bird, the burning tree;
Innocent of their state, the poets wander,
Seeking the kindred of their incarnation,
Waste land and homeless sea.
Phosphor declining as Orion rises
May for a brief hour break his isolation,
The dying Phoenix see
New Phoenix blazing in her nest of spices.

Only in space, not time, the pattern changes:
Over your land of memory, enchanted
Glides the Celestial Swan, and in your bitter
Darkness the She-Bear shambles round the Pole;
Anvils of summer, in mine, the iron ranges
Rise from its arid heart to see the haunted
River of Light unroll
Towards Achernar, where Hermes, the transmitter
Of spirits, herald of men and gods, has granted
Speech between soul and soul,
And each to each the Swan and Phoenix glitter.

The mortal hearts of poets first engender
The parleying of those immortal creatures;
Then from their interchange create unending
Orbits of song and colloquies of light;
Sexes in their apocalyptic splendour
In mutual contemplation of their natures
Transfigure or unite;

Descant and burden in diapason blending,
Urania dances, and the sacred gestures
  Become the words we write,
My lark arising or your dove descending.

For you the gods of song forgo their quarrel;
Panther and Wolf forget their former anger;
For you this ancient ceremony of greeting
Becomes a solemn apopemptic hymn.
Muses who twine the ivy with the laurel
In savage measures celebrate you, Stranger;
  For you the Maenads trim
Their torches and, in order due repeating
The stately ode, invoke you. Wanderer, Ranger,
  Beyond the utmost rim
Of waters, hear the voice of these entreating!

And, as the solitary bird of passage,
Loosing her heart across the wastes of ocean,
Sees round the cliffs of home the black tide crawling,
Accept the incantation of this verse;
Read its plain words; divine the secret message
By which the dance itself reveals a notion
  That moves our universe.
In the star rising or the lost leaf falling
The life of poetry, this enchanted motion,
  Perpetually recurs.
Take, then, this homage of our craft and calling!

Put on your figures of fable: with the chalice
From which the poets alone drink wisdom, healing
And joy that weds the thyrsus with the lyre,
Be Circe—or be my Queen of Sheba; come
Silent at nightfall to my silent palace

And read my heart, and rest; and when the wheeling
  Signs of the sky turn home,
I shall arise and show you in his byre
Among your milk-white dromedaries kneeling,
  Fierce in that lilied gloom,
My horn of gold, my unicorn of fire.

THE FAREWELL

Here's to you, all you ladies
That lie upon the town,
Whose pleasure and whose trade is
To romp on beds of down.
On beds of down reclining
You rest the livelong day,
And when the stars are shining
Begin your wanton play.

And here's to all your lovers
For whom you ply the trade,
The beds beneath whose covers
The gallant game is played,
The girdles and the laces
That dress your silken thighs
And those enchanting graces
That catch us with surprise.

And here's to you, my dearest,
The queen of all their crew,
The wisest and the fairest,
I take my leave of you.

The feast is done, the table
Is bare, the night grows old;
Your voice concludes the fable
That cannot be retold.

As once you gave me warning,
When close with you I lay,
To leave you ere the dawning,
See, now it is the day!
And you it was who taught me
I must expect its light
To quench the stars that brought me
Along the road of night.

So fare you well, you ladies
That warmed me with your fires;
A sun that casts no shade is
What now my soul requires.
Well seasoned is the timber
I brought you green, and yet
Lord! how my bones remember
The things they should forget!

Farewell the kind embraces
In which my heart grew wise,
A keener light replaces
The brilliance of your eyes.
Farewell the school of pleasure
In which I studied long.
I tread a graver measure,
But learn a sweeter song.

THE WALKER

Who walks round my house all night?
None but lanky Tom.

AN OLD CHILDREN'S GAME

Who walks round my house all night,
Stepping sad and slow,
Ghost or woman, child or sprite?
None that I do know.

Who is she that haunts the dark
When the moon is down,
Street or garden, pale or park,
Through the sleeping town?

When the frost falls thick and chill
And the stars slide by,
In my bed I hear it still,
Hear her walk and sigh.

Sultry midnights when I wake
In the clutch of fear,
Though my bones with fever shake,
Nothing do I hear;

Nothing, nothing can I spy
Through the darkened pane;
Yet, when on my bed I lie,
Come those steps again;

Comes the sound of mortal grief
And the tread of woe—
Is it woman, spirit, thief,
Pacing to and fro?

"Lover, keep your careless bed,
Turn you to the wall.
Not the living, not the dead
Answers here your call;

"But a witness from the void,
Banned with drug and knife,
Whom your coward heart destroyed
In the gates of life."

THE WATCHER

Can the tree that grows in grief
Rooted in its own despair
Crown its head with bud and leaf,
Blossom and enrich the air?

Can the bird that on the bough
Tries the ripeness of the fruit,
Taste the agony below,
Know the worm that cuts the root?

In a dream I saw my tree
Clothed in paradisal white,
Every branch in ecstasy
Spread its odours on the night;

Lovers walking two and two
Felt their own delight expressed,
And the bird that thither flew
Chose its branches for her nest;

Children in a laughing tide
Thronged it round to taste and see;
"See the shining fruit," they cried,
"See the happy, blossoming tree!"

You alone among them there
Came with your divining heart,
Breathed that still, enchanted air,
Felt your tears in anguish start,

And the passion of your woe
At the sweetness of the fruit
Watered all the ground below,
Touched and healed the wounded root.

Then the bird among the leaves
Checked its song in sad surmise;
Then the lover saw what grieves
In the depths of human eyes;

But the children at your side
Took your hands and laughed to see
"O the shining fruit," they cried,
"O the happy, happy tree!"

AGONY COLUMN

Sir George and Lady Cepheus of Upper Slaughter
Desire to announce to family and friends
That the death has been arranged of their only daughter
Andromeda, aged twenty—Sir George intends

To avoid undesirable pomp and ostentation:
A simple ceremony, a quiet funeral feast
And the usual speeches; a train will leave the station
For the Virgin's Rock at four. No flowers by Request!

Owing to the informal nature of the occasion
Guests are requested to wear ordinary dress.
It is hoped that, in view of Sir George's official station
The event will be treated discreetly by the press.

In accord with religious custom and public duty,
The populace is expected to maintain order and quiet;
But, because of her daughter's quite exceptional beauty
And numerous suitors, to discourage scandal or riot,

Lady Cepheus wishes it to be distinctly stated
That any attempt at rescue has been banned;
Offenders will be summarily emasculated;
Heroes are warned: the police have the matter in hand.

As the victim is to be chained wearing only her skin,
The volunteer armorers will be blinded at once.
On the following morning her lovers and next-of-kin
May assist in gathering any remaining bones.

LAMBKIN: A FABLE

A Lamb, that had gone much astray,
Among the mountains lost his way;
His heart, his fleece, alike were black;
He staggered on the stony track;
Grim cliffs and crags above him towered;
Below the precipices loured;
The eagles watching from the height
Observed: "He will be ours by night",
And, as he reached the line of snow,
Night gathered in the vale below.
The cold was fierce, the barren pass
Scarce offered him one blade of grass.
Alone, unshepherded, his state
Was little less than desperate,
As down he laid his aching bones
Among the hard, unmothering stones,
And on that bleak and bitter air
Bleated a chance, belated prayer.

What was his joy—he lay in doubt—
His bleat was answered by a shout!
Feebly he rose and answered back:
A cheerful hail rang up the track,
And soon, quite safe from hurts and harms,
He lay in the Good Shepherd's arms.

Through the long hours of dark, as they
Towards the fold retraced their way,
He wept indeed, but not for shame
To view the wicked way he came,
Nor fear to meet the master's wrath
Threatened upon his setting forth,

Nor keen repentance at his fall,
But joy to be alive at all.

And yet his tears, as is the case
When the heart turns and cries for grace,
Availed him more than he could know
And washed his black soul white as snow.
At length the weary way was done
Just at the rising of the sun,
And, issuing from a bleak defile,
They saw the dewy pastures smile,
The sheep-cotes and the homely fold,
The crested mountains touched with gold.
And, when he was set down at last,
A sudden tremor through him passed,
For lo, his fleece, once black as night,
Was now a pure and dazzling white!

Who now so glad as Lambkin? Who
Resolved to make his life anew?
The same dull round from day to day
He trod and found it fresh and gay;
No task too hard, no toil too long:
"My pains are given to make me strong."
Such inward, burning joy to feel
Made him the paragon of zeal;
And then the Shepherd, always near,
Would fondle him and smile to hear
His children pat and pet and praise
The Lamb who learned to mend his ways.
So Lambkin felt as good as gold.
Alas, he found within the fold,
Among his fellow tups and ewes,
Less disposition to enthuse;

For when they greeted him their eyes
Showed neither scandal nor surprise;
They did not seem impressed to learn
His perils or his safe return,
And some were even heard to say:
"Why, Lambkin, have you been away?"
His deadly sins, this new-won grace
That made his such a special case
Alike ignored, he felt his fall
Had scarcely been remarked at all.

No matter! Fire-new virtue asks
Increasing tests and heavier tasks;
The soul unproved can still invent
Worse trials than those by Heaven sent
And finds, of all, the hardest part
To humble the too-eager heart.
So Lambkin found. Though not content,
He bore his modest punishment,
Yet still contrived with Heaven's decrees
To dot the i's and cross the t's.
First at the Shepherd's call and first
Afield, he always chose the worst
And rankest pasture; at the pool
Drank last his muddy belly-full.
When other lambs were at their pranks,
He cropped beside his parents' flanks;
Spied the wolf's ears behind the rock
And was the first to warn the flock;
On dog-days chose the scantiest shade;
Faced drench and tailing unafraid
And for the shearing nursed his wool:
"Lord, help me make it Three Bags Full!"

Alas for virtue and for zeal!
As summer passed, he came to feel,
Compared with him, his fellow sheep
Too much inclined to sloth and sleep.
The Nine and Ninety, faithful crew,
Though they were guiltless, it was true,
Had never strayed, would not rebel,
Were somewhat slack in doing well.
Afold the wethers would complain
Of wind and dust, or mud and rain;
Afield the ewes would criticize
The sheep-dog's temper, or the flies;
The rams were prone, in good or bad,
To take for granted what they had;
And all complained with ill-concealed
Annoyance, when he led the field:
"Go easy; do you have to trot?
Lambkin, you make the pace too hot!"

"My friends," he answered them at last,
"The time for diffidence is past.
The crimes for which I now atone,
My shame and guilt, I freely own;
And I, the least among you here,
Would hold my peace, did I not fear
That even while I hesitate
To warn you, it may be too late.
Unworthy as I am and weak,
Hear, then, what conscience bids me speak:

"My tale, as most of you should know,
Begins one day six months ago
When, black without and foul within,
Leprous and ulcerate with sin,

The Shepherd snatched me, ere I fell,
Back from the very brink of Hell.
O for a tongue that could express
That moment of pure happiness!
Once more within the fold I stood,
Renewed by Grace, redeemed by Blood.
At first with tears I viewed the place
And every dear, familiar face;
It seemed, through dim and weeping eyes,
A little short of Paradise.
But soon, forgive if I speak plain,
My tears were dry; I looked again.
This fold, which seemed at first so fair,
Had an ill-kept, neglected air;
The troughs were split, the stalls awry,
Through crazy timbers showed the sky;
Sheep-tods and puddles on the floor
And tailings mixed with shabby straw;
The lambs unruly, and the ewes
Gossips too apt to air their views;
The wethers envious of the tups;
The rams vainglorious in their cups;
The watch-dog slack; the sheep-dog sly;
Bedraggled wool and udders dry—
Such was the picture; and—I blame
My silence—it is still the same.

"You do not see it thus, 'tis true;
You could not be expected to.
Habit is strong and makes us blind.
Indeed, though it may seem unkind
To mention this, there have been times
When I have almost blessed the crimes

Which, deadly as they are, may be
A means of Grace to make us see.

"There have been times when I have stood
Chewing my conscientious cud,
Erect, to save this spotless fleece,
While in the dust you took your ease
Careless of dirt and keds and burrs,
When I have wondered: was it worse
To stay at home or to rebel?
Or was I even—who can tell?—
Upon that dark and fatal day
Led providentially astray?

"We are but sheep, and as we can
Must strive to guess the Shepherd's plan;
And yet, what other can it be
Than this: to touch your hearts through *me*?
Look, then, on me and rise and shine
And win a fleece as white as mine!"

The words were scarcely out before
First smiles, then sniggers, then a roar
Of helpless laughter shook the fold.
Again it rose; again it rolled,
While Lambkin, taken by surprise,
Stared back with grieved and puzzled eyes;
And next chagrin, and last dismay
Possessed him, and he ran away.

Away! Still followed by their rude,
Hilarious ingratitude,
He passed the mustering pens, the race,
The shearing shed, and none gave chase.
No voice behind cried: "Lambkin, wait!"

He reached the open pasture gate
And passed the empty fields, and took
A sheep-pad leading to the brook;
And, stooping to the pool, he saw
What all the merriment was for:
The face reflected in the pool
Was his, and his for sure the wool,
Except that all he viewed below
Showed black as pitch from top to toe.

MAN FRIDAY

For John Pringle

Saved at long last through Him whose power to save
Kept from the walking, as the watery grave,
Crusoe returned to England and his kind,
Proof that an unimaginative mind
And sober industry and common sense
May supplement the work of Providence.
He, no less providential, and no less
Inscrutably resolved to save and bless,
Eager to share his fortune with the weak
And faithful servants whom he taught to speak,
By all his years of exile undeterred,
Took into exile Friday and the bird.

The bird no doubt was well enough content.
She had her corn—what matter where she went?
Except when once a week he walked to church,
She had her master's shoulder as a perch,

She shared the notice of the crowds he drew
Who praised her language and her plumage too,
And like a rational female could be gay
On admiration and three meals a day.

But Friday, the dark Caribbean man,
Picture his situation if you can:
The gentle savage, taught to speak and pray,
On England's Desert Island cast away,
No godlike Crusoe issuing from his cave
Comes with his thunderstick to slay and save;
Instead from caves of stone, as thick as trees,
More dreadful than ten thousand savages,
In their strange clothes and monstrous mats of hair,
The pale-eyed English swarm to joke and stare,
With endless questions round him crowd and press
Curious to see and touch his loneliness.
Unlike his master Crusoe long before
Crawling half-drowned upon the desolate shore,
Mere ingenuity useless in his need,
No wreck supplies him biscuit, nails and seed,
No fort to build, no call to bake, to brew,
Make pots and pipkins, cobble coat and shoe,
Gather his rice and milk his goats, and rise
Daily to some absorbing enterprise.

And yet no less than Crusoe he must find
Some shelter for the solitary mind;
Some daily occupation to contrive
To warm his wits and keep the heart alive;
Protect among the cultured, if he can,
The "noble savage" and the "natural man".
As Crusoe made his clothes, so he no less
Must labour to invent his nakedness

And, lest their alien customs without trace
Absorb him, tell the legends of his race
Each night aloud in the soft native tongue,
That filled his world when, bare and brown and young,
His brown, bare mother held him at her breast,
Then say his English prayers and sink to rest.
And each day waking in his English sheets,
Hearing the wagons in the cobbled streets,
The morning bells, the clatter and cries of trade,
He must recall, within their palisade,
The sleeping cabins in the tropic dawn,
The rapt, leaf-breathing silence, and the yawn
Of naked children as they wake and drowse,
The women chattering round their fires, the prows
Of wet canoes nosing the still lagoon;
At each meal, handling alien fork or spoon,
Remember the spiced mess of yam and fish
And the brown fingers meeting in the dish;
Remember too those island feasts, the sweet
Blood frenzy and the taste of human meat.

Thus he piled memories against his need:
In vain! For still he found the past recede.
Try as he would, recall, relive, rehearse,
The cloudy images would still disperse,
Till, as in dreams, the island world he knew
Confounded the fantastic with the true,
While England, less unreal day by day,
The Cannibal Island, ate his past away.
But for the brooding eye, the swarthy skin,
That witnessed to the Natural Man within,
Year following year, by inches, as they ran,
Transformed the savage to an Englishman.
Brushed, barbered, hatted, trousered and baptized,

He looked, if not completely civilized,
What came increasingly to be the case:
An upper servant, conscious of his place,
Friendly but not familiar in address
And prompt to please, without obsequiousness,
Adept to dress, to shave, to carve, to pour
And skilled to open or refuse the door,
To keep on terms with housekeeper and cook,
But quell the maids and footmen with a look.
And now his master, thoughtful for his need,
Bought him a wife and gave him leave to breed.
A fine mulatto, once a lady's maid,
She thought herself superior to Trade
And, reared on a Plantation, much too good
For a low native Indian from the wood;
Yet they contrived at last to rub along
For he was strong and kind, and she was young,
And soon a father, then a family man,
Friday took root in England and began
To be well thought of in the little town,
And quoted in discussions at "The Crown",
Whether the Funds would fall, the French would treat
Or the new ministry could hold its seat.
For though he seldom spoke, the rumour ran
The master had no secrets from his man,
And Crusoe's ventures prospered so, in short,
It was concluded he had friends at Court.

Yet as the years of exile came and went,
Though first he grew resigned and then content,
Had you observed him close, you might surprise
A stranger looking through the servant's eyes.
Some colouring of speech, some glint of pride,
Not born of hope, for hope long since had died,

Not even desire, scarce memory at last,
Preserved that stubborn vestige of the past.

It happened once that man and master made
A trip together on affairs of trade;
A ship reported foundered in the Downs
Brought them to visit several seaport towns.
At one of these, Great Yarmouth or King's Lynn,
Their business done, they baited at an inn,
And in the night were haunted by the roar
Of a wild wind and tide against the shore.
Crusoe soon slept again, but Friday lay
Awake and listening till the dawn of day.
For the first time in all his exiled years
The thunder of the ocean filled his ears;
And that tremendous voice so long unheard
Released and filled and drew him, till he stirred
And left the house and passed the town, to reach
At last the dunes and rocks and open beach:
Pale, bare and gleaming in the break of day
A sweep of new-washed sand around the bay,
And spindrift driving up the bluffs like smoke,
As the long combers reared their crests and broke.
There in the sand beside him Friday saw
A single naked footprint on the shore.
His heart stood still, for as he stared, he knew
The foot that made it never had worn shoe
And, at a glance, that no such walker could
Have been a man of European blood.
From such a footprint once he could describe
If not the owner's name, at least his tribe,
And tell his purpose as men read a face
And still his skill sufficed to know the race;
For this was such a print as long ago

He too had made and taught his eyes to know.
There could be no mistake. Awhile he stood
Staring at that grey German Ocean's flood;
And suddenly he saw those shores again
Where Orinoco pours into the main,
And, stunned with an incredible surmise,
Heard in his native tongue once more the cries
Of spirits silent now for many a day;
And all his years of exile fell away.

The sun was nearly to the height before
Crusoe arrived hallooing at the shore,
Followed the footprints to the beach and found
The clothes and shoes and thought his servant drowned.
Much grieved he sought him up and down the bay
But never guessed, when later in the day
They found the body drifting in the foam,
That Friday had been rescued and gone home.

A BIDDING GRACE

For what we are about to hear, Lord, Lord,
The dreadful judgement, the unguessed reprieve,
The brief, the battering, the jubilant chord
Of trumpets quickening this guilty dust,
Which still would hide from what it shall receive,
Lord, make us thankful to be what we must.

For what we are now about to lose, reprove,
Assuage or comfort, Lord, this greedy flesh,
Still grieving, still rebellious, still in love,
Still prodigal of treasure still unspent.
Teach the blood weaving through its intricate mesh
The sigh, the solace, the silence of consent.

For what we are about to learn too late, too late
To save, though we repent with tears of blood:
The innocent ruined, the gentle taught to hate,
The love we made a means to its despair—
For all we have done or did not when we could,
Redouble on us the evil these must bear.

For what we are about to say, urge, plead,
The specious argument, the lame excuse,
Prompt our contempt. When these archangels read
Our trivial balance, lest the shabby bill
Tempt to that abjectness which begs or sues,
Leave us one noble impulse: to be still.

For what we are about to act, the lust, the lie
That works unbidden, even now restrain
This reckless heart. Though doomed indeed to die,
Grant that we may, still trembling at the bar
Of Justice in the thud of fiery rain,
Acknowledge at last the truth of what we are.

In all we are about to receive, last, last,
Lord, help us bear our part with all men born
And, after judgement given and sentence passed,
Even at this uttermost, measured in thy gaze,
Though in thy mercy, for the rest to mourn,
Though in thy wrath we stand, to stand and praise.

A LETTER FROM ROME

For Dr Leonie Kramer

Rome, Rome! thou art no more
As thou has been!

FELICIA HEMANS

Hotel della Rotonda
ROME 1958

Man being transitory likes to act
As though he had all time to air his views.
Man being idle takes to rhyme. In fact
Journeying in the company of the Muse,
I'd just arrived at this hotel, unpacked,
Refurbished, washed my face and changed my shoes,
When in she came all smiles and said: "In Rome,
The thing to do is, write a letter home."

"My dear, good girl," I said, "do you forget a
Theme like this needs eagle wings to soar?
I might just rise to a familiar letter,
News, observations, gossip, nothing more.
Besides, it's all been done and done much better;
I've never tried that sort of thing before.
Australian poets, you recall, prefer
The packhorse and the slip-rail and the spur."

"High time they stopped it then," the Muse replied,
"I never liked that pioneering strain,
The tales of how those mountain horsemen ride—
Today they drive a truck or take a plane.

Australian poets, if they ever tried,
Might show at least a rudiment of brain,
And yours—" "All right," I answered with a grin,
"You've talked me into it, my dear; you win!"

So here I am in the Eternal City
The Pantheon itself is just next door.
I might be wise, I might at least be witty
Where bards have been so eloquent before.
Some found her splendid, others thought her pretty,
Some said she was the Babylonian Whore;
But each was vocal, *vehemens et tremens*,
From Roman Virgil down to Mrs Hemans.

Yet travelling poets, even at the best,
Are apt to turn out bores or something worse;
Even *Childe Harold*, it must be confessed,
Is sometimes merely Baedeker in verse,
And for a new antipodean guest
Rome as a subject daunts, if not deters.
But I, since she demands my tribute, can
At least contrive to write some lines that scan;

And since I'm launched now in *ottava rima*,
—For easy-going verse it's just the thing—
I shan't attempt the high poetic theme or
Pitch my note to make the welkin ring.
That "*Roma non è più come era prima*"
Which Byron heard the Roman workmen sing
Gives scope to write on anything at all
Since Romulus and Remus built their wall.

I might compile a *Muses' Guide to Rome*,
Describing all the sights and trips and treats,

Label the cells that cram the honeycomb,
The haunts of poets and their favourite streets,
The gate where Ovid lingered leaving home,
The oak of Tasso and the tomb of Keats,
The booth where Horace bought Falernian wine,
The restaurant where Goethe used to dine.

I have just dined myself extremely well
And drunk much wine, though not Falernian.
I might, if I were Goethe, who can tell,
Compose a new *West-Oestliche Diwan*,
Like Mrs Browning I might raise from hell
A Vision of the Poets, man by man,
And show you who was who, and what was what;
But something warns me I had better not.

A man, of course, should know his limitations
And, only if he has one, trust his star.
But poets ought to risk their reputations
To find out what those limitations are;
And modern poets put me out of patience
Wanting the grace, or guts, to aim too far.
So in this instance I shall *not* proceed
To emulate the Venerable Bede.

Just think of Bede the Tourist!—I, you see, am
Not drunk, but just a little "flown with wine"—
Bede came to Rome and offered his Te Deum,
Fresh from a land as barbarous as mine,
Made one remark about the Colosseum
And plodded back to Jarrow-on-the-Tyne.
And think of Bede the Poet, satisfied
To leave *one* poem, composed the day he died!

But lacking Bede's restraint, I must beware
In Rome the pilgrim's more besetting sin,
Which made poor Mistress Kempe so hard to bear,
God's holy howler-monkey from King's Lynn,
Too much engrossed in Margery Kempe to spare
A page to the great city she was in,
For here I am with eighty lines set down
About myself and eight about the town.

So to my theme—and if I should digress,
As possibly I shall do by and by,
Skip as you please; most readers do, I guess,
Faced with the longer forms of poetry.
If I run on, one reason, I confess,
Is to employ the tongue and rest the eye:
Six weeks a tourist render me, alas,
As blind as Balaam, chattier than his ass.

The Tourist's fate though curiously reversed
Is that of Tantalus who watched a feast
Devoured by famine, who, consumed by thirst
Saw the cool waters rising to his breast.
The tourist has to cram until he burst
Or gulp until he vomit like a beast;
But either way the case is much the same;
The arrows of desire miss their aim.

Six weeks in Italy! He has to grapple
With all the culture that there is to see
In baptistery, temple, church or chapel,
Museum, mausoleum, gallery.
Adam was cursed for eating that one apple,
But had he finished the whole fatal tree
He might have found that gorging Good and Evil
Led less to Sin and Death than mere upheaval.

If asked to sink too fast too many bumpers,
No matter how felicitous the wine,
The mental belly will begin a rumpus
No matter though the matter is divine.
There is an end to what the eye can compass
Of perfect colour and superb design,
And whether art be sacred or profane,
To look too often is to look in vain.

Day after day, with guide-book at the ready,
I've stormed the galleries from hall to hall,
Where headless muse or mutilated lady
Are flanked by god unsexed or Dying Gaul.
Checking my members every night in bed, I
Have groaned, I must admit, as I recall
That on the morrow waits for me a fresh
Mountain of marble chiselled into flesh.

I've contemplated all the types of Venus
Which win the heart or take the soul by storm,
The modest fig-leaf and the shameless penis
In every proper or improper form,
Until the individual in the genus
Is lost and all exceptions in the norm,
And fair and foul and quaint and crass and crude
Dissolve in one vast cliché of the Nude.

I've seen enough Nativities to fluster
The whole collective Midwives' Fellowship,
More angels than scholastic wits could thrust a
Pin between, or count upon the tip,
More Virgins than St Ursula could muster

To chaperon that fatal one-way trip,
And Holy Families and Annunciations
By tribes and hordes and multitudes and nations.

I've viewed the pitch of human ingenuity
Record in bronze, in marble and in paint
New schemes and still new schemes in perpetuity
For martyrdoms—and some extremely quaint—
New ways to grill St Lawrence, if to do it he
Were forced to spatchcock that devoted saint,
New ways to stick Sebastian full of arrows
And scarify St What's-his-name with harrows.

Augustine possibly was optimistic
About the rout and ruin of pagan gods;
The City of God, triumphant book, was his stick,
The City of Rome had always other rods,
And Christian savages, no less sadistic
Than those who at the Circus had laid odds
Upon the lion and against the martyr
Now took their pleasures in another quarter.

I grant the butchery of the arena
Was finished and the bad old days were done;
But brothers of the wolf and the hyena
Could still contrive to have their grisly fun;
Where painter vied with painter to give keener
Edge to the axe, make bloodier rivers run,
It gave a thrill as brutal, though vicarious,
To lop Eulalia or chop Januarius.

Yet saint or sadist, each could gaze his fill
Or if unfilled, come back another day.
Before a masterpiece the mind could still

Take time to learn, to ponder or to pray.
The modern tourist pays a job-lot bill,
Takes one quick look and then is whisked away:
"Next we see Titian's famous—Ah, too late!
Alas, messieurs, mesdames, our bus won't wait."

The Muses have no schedules, they are free,
But foreign travel, once a private venture
At best, is now a major industry
Where dividend and bonus and debenture,
Compete with wisdom, love and piety.
Change them for comfort, uplift, tame adventure,
And those who put a girdle round the earth
Will guarantee we get our money's worth.

The pilgrims of the age of faith bareshod
Tramped across Europe, singing by the way;
Innkeepers, robbers on the roads they trod
Might wait and make of them their natural prey;
And Rome once reached, the ministers of God
For each act of devotion make them pay;
But no one sold them "culture" on the side
Or made them beggars to his Barmecide.

Romantic Felicaja! He was sure
His country had her scenery to thank
For all invasions, Lombard, Goth and Moor,
German and Spaniard, Saracen and Frank;
"The fatal gift of beauty", not the lure
Of rape, the simple urge to rob a bank,
Or what impels a Mohawk to take scalps,
Had led them up her coasts or through the Alps.

It was quite other armies the reward
Of Beauty drew—it draws them to this day—
The travelling gentleman, the young milord,
Hell-bent on culture, curios, women, play,
Drank, diced and duelled, dug for statues, whored,
Bought pictures or sketched ruins, came away
At last complete, accomplished, finished fellows,
Formed by her courts or poxed by her bordellos.

And after the Grand Tour there came the Trip
Abroad, a much more middle-class affair:
Migratory bards recovering from the pip,
The family party, the adulterous pair,
The archaeologists in a chartered ship,
Lounged, ate *gelati*, swam or stopped to stare
At Ruskin sketching every stone in Venice
Or Browning in his braces playing tennis.

Well "culture" in the eighties, at a guess,
Did little harm. As far as one can see,
Seasons in Italy were more or less
A leisured picnic, a light-hearted spree.
That dogged transatlantic earnestness
From which no nation now on earth is free,
Had not yet turned its pleasure into solemn
Lectures on how to look at Trajan's column.

It soon came on, indeed was on the way,
As Henry James depicted it, for one.
In any picture-gallery today
Kulturgeschichte takes away the fun
Unless one joins a group and cares to stay
To watch the Herr Professor toss the bun
To teach us peasants, munching it with zeal,
Not only what to think but how to feel.

However lucid, well-informed, vivacious
The lecturer's task is hopeless from the start:
Most ready-made emotions are fallacious
And there's no ready-made response to art.
Tibetan prayer-wheels may be efficacious
Since those who twirl them know the prayers by heart,
But these are devotees whose utmost skill
Consists in knowing how to gulp the pill.

Of course it would be stupid out of measure
To laugh at those who know their need to learn.
For some, perhaps, who never had the leisure
Nor yet the chance before, this serves their turn.
A tale I heard last week with simple pleasure
In Florence dots the i's of my concern,
And illustrates to what absurd degree
Some people will proceed to cross a t.

That evening I had dinner with a man
Who has lived forty years in Italy,
Half English, more than half Italian
With all the latter's gift of irony;
And while we drank our wine my host began
To talk of Florence and her history,
Her life, her people, and to finish off he
Told me the following story over coffee:

"In Florence there is a well-known foundation,
Richly endowed from the United States,
Trimmed to the latest trends in education,
It 'finishes' young women graduates
And gives them poise and polish for the station
Their family's bank-balance indicates,
The sort of thing entitled, as a rule,
A Continental Summer Graduate School.

"Its aims are serious, its methods sound,
Its courses academically respectable,
Fine Arts for those who like to shop around,
Western Philosophy for the directable,
And Poetry from Poe to Ezra Pound,
With, just to stiffen subjects so delectable,
A weekly seminar, a monthly test,
And Love is on the course with all the rest.

"Of course it is not on their syllabus,
As best confined to individual choice;
But hints are dropped in sessions to discuss
How to attain maturity and poise
That, if arranged discreetly, without fuss,
Brief love-affairs with nice Italian boys
May well repay the trouble and expense
Since nothing broadens like experience.

"Italian boys are not, and never were,
Averse to girls when rich, well-dressed and pretty.
The summer school created quite a stir
Among the young Lotharios of the city;
The alleys throbbed with an expectant purr;
The streets were filled with amorous banditti.
The girls of Florence, it may be, were less
Well-pleased, but that is anybody's guess.

"But how to set about it? How to find
A lover? That's quite simple in a town
Where every girl gets pinched on the behind
In shops, trams, church, or walking up and down.
It's half an invitation, half a kind

Of compliment. If she should turn and frown
That's that; but if she smiles, he'll raise his hat
And ask her to take coffee, and that's *that!*

"Louise, though very beautiful, was what I'm
Inclined to call a serious girl at heart,
And, though endowed with an attractive bottom,
Thought pinching it no proper way to start;
And Alessandro was well-bred; if not I'm
Sure he knew just how to act the part.
He met her at a concert, did not pinch,
But said the *pizzicati* made him flinch.

"She smiled and said: 'How's that?' The ice was broken.
He offered coffee. She did not refuse.
They talked on various topics which betoken
The parties each have cultivated views.
And as they talked their eyes said things unspoken.
The world was all before them, where to choose.
He saw her home and on the doorstep they
Arranged to meet again the following day.

"Louise went in and calmly jotted down
Some notes on her emotional reactions,
Removed her make-up, donned her dressing gown
And nicely planned her conduct and her actions;
While Alessandro wandered through the town
Enraptured by her charms and her attractions.
His plans were just the usual well-bred
Young man's to get the girl to go to bed.

"To his surprise, and more to his chagrin,
She went to bed without the least demur.
Passion expects resistance, and to win
Without it, on his passion cast a slur.

He loved her voice, her eyes, her shape, her skin
But found no answering response in her.
She loved him, not for love however fiery,
But for providing data for her diary.

"They went to bed; they took a trip to Pisa;
They 'did' the Pitti; and they went to bed;
She told him all about herself; to please her
He talked about Etruscan tombs; she read
Her diary to him and that day to ease a
Sense of strain they took a walk instead;
They walked, they talked, she reasoned and he swore,
But in the end they went to bed once more.

"And at the close of a divine semester
She annotated and revised her notes,
Wrote: 'Field-Work' on the cover and repressed a
Less serious urge to label it: 'Wild Oats'.
She can't say Europe very much impressed her,
Though Sandro is a name on which she dotes.
She thinks that Kinsey overrates the male."
And here my host broke off his merry tale.

A Merry Tale? Boccaccio might have written:
"How Messer Sandro wooed a learnèd dame,
But found his labour lost, the biter bitten
And half a thesis cooked upon his flame."
Yet I am sad to see so many smitten
By the same view of art and much the same
Approach as this poor girl's who thought her fee
Made Love one more post-graduate degree.

But talking of degrees, the Schedule Beaters
On any scale of nonsense touch the top.

Hung round with cameras, light-filters, metres,
Always on time and travelling till they drop,
They pause—a wife identifies St Peter's.
They never look at all, but make a stop,
Squint, fiddle, click and, happy, hurry back
To Bristol, Cincinnati or Toorak.

Watching these futile pilgrims in their legions
Who must get home to find where they have been,
I find myself who owe them no allegiance,
Caught in a farce as senseless as obscene,
Asking what brings *me* here from those dim regions
Where Dante planted Hell's Back Door, and Dean
Swift his microcosm of civilization?
The facts fell short of their imagination

For I am no infernal refugee
And reach a normal height of five foot nine.
Yet there *is* something strange, I would agree,
In those dumb continents below the Line.
The roots are European, but the tree
Grows to a different pattern and design;
Where the fruit gets its flavour I'm not sure,
From native soil or overseas manure.

And this uncertainty is in our bones.
Others may think us smug or insular;
The voice perhaps is brash, its undertones
Declare in us a doubt of what we are.
When the divided ghost within us groans
It must return to find its avatar.
Though this puts things too solemnly, of course,
Yet here am I returning to the source.

That source is Italy, and hers is Rome,
The *fons et origo* of Western Man;
Athens perhaps begot, Rome was the womb;
Here the great venture of the heart began.
Here simply with a sense of coming home
I have returned with no explicit plan
Beyond a child's uncertain quest, to find
Something once dear, long lost and left behind.

The clue lies not in art or history,
Relics or ruins that survive their prime.
The thing I came to find was lost in *me*,
Not in the Forum's dust, the Tiber's slime.
The act which resurrects is just to be
Patient before these witnesses of time.
The graves may open and their dead appear,
But mine is the sepulchral voice I hear.

The efficacy of place, like that of prayer,
Lies in no overt effort of the will;
To keep the mind unquesting but aware,
The heart unmoving but responsive still,
Opens the way to forces which prepare
Answers whose questions lie beyond our skill,
And this, I know, is what I have in view,
As other poets, I think, have felt it too.

And one especially is in my mind:
The limping man, the legend of his age.
Asking myself what *he* came here to find
I've just re-read *Childe Harold's Pilgrimage*,
Which offers, almost equally combined,
The shrewd, the silly, the noble and the sage,
The stamp of genius and the touch of sham.
Well, I'm quite sure of one thing: that I am

Not like the Pilgrim of Eternity,
Revisiting the Muses' Campo Santo,
Not like his Harold—who indeed could be
Like Harold, and what man alive would want to?
Yet what moved Byron then, it seems to me,
To write his fourth, superb and final canto,
Impels me too to write, although the scene
Is somewhat changed since eighteen seventeen.

What caused him to leave Venice? Well, he said
He'd like to take a trip and see the Pope,
Hinted he'd like a rest from too much bed
With a blonde charmer called the Antelope;
Writing to Murray for tooth-powder (red)
He said that Rome had drawn him with the hope
To make Constantinople's glories pale.
The poem, I think, tells quite another tale.

Unlike that desultory scenic stroll
Which robs his earlier cantos of their force,
This moves, with sure direction and control,
In towards the centre, back towards the source.
Its theme is destiny and Rome its goal;
And yet it does not stop with Rome; the course
Of history retraced, it moves at last
Into the savage, pre-historic past.

It ends with Nemi and the Golden Bough.
What instinct led him there? I like to think
What drew him then is what has drawn me now
To stand in time upon that timeless brink,
To sense there the renewal of a vow,

The mending of a lost primordial link.
These may be only fancies, yet I swear
I felt the presence of the numen there.

There's nothing now at Nemi to evoke
Sir James G. Frazer's memorable scene:
The sleepless victim-King, the sacred oak;
A market garden spreads its tidy green
Where stood Diana's grove; no voices spoke;
There were no omens; cloudless and serene
The sun beat harshly on the drowsing lake;
And yet I felt my senses wide awake,

Alert, expectant—as we scrambled down
The crater from the village to the shore
And strolled along its path, we were alone;
And, picnicking among the rocks, I saw
No cause for these sensations. Yet I own
A tension grew upon me more and more.
What Byron felt as calm and cherished hate
For me was more like force, insistence, fate.

And under this impulsion from the place,
I seemed constrained, before I came to drink,
To pour some wine upon the water's face,
Later, to strip and wade out from the brink.
Was it a plea for chrism or for grace?
An expiation? More than these, I think
I was possessed, and what possessed me there
Was Europe's oldest ritual of prayer.

But prayer to whom, for what? The Intervention
Did not reveal itself or what it meant.
The body simply prays without "intention",

The mind by the bare force of its assent.
That "higher, more extended comprehension",
Which Byron, writing after the event,
Felt necessary to explain brute fact,
Came by mere power of my consenting act.

Well, let it pass: I have no views about it;
Only I sensed some final frontier passed,
Some seed, long dormant, which has stirred and sprouted,
Some link of understanding joined at last.
I may have been deluded, but I doubt it
Though where the series leads I can't forecast.
Laugh at these intimations if you will;
The days go by and they are with me still.

Meanwhile I walk and gaze. For all its size,
Rome is a city one can see on foot,
And that's the pace for such an enterprise.
Each morning we buy cheese and rolls and fruit
And stroll and stop to view whatever lies
Along a vague and ambulating route.
I miss a lot of course, but what I see,
Because *I* found it, seems a part of *me*.

And as I walk I think of my own land
To which I must return when this trip's over.
She speaks a language that I understand,
And wakes no love that "moves with the remover".
I fear this letter's getting out of hand
But there's a topic still I wish to cover
Which hangs upon a tale of Yin and Yang:
The *Abendland*'s reputed *Untergang*.

I'd like to say at once I've never much
Believed the prophets of impending doom,
The Spenglers, T. S. Eliots and such,
Guides to the Waste Lands and the Wrath to Come.
Perhaps I'm simply rather out of touch,
But I'm confirmed by what I sense in Rome.
She still is *urbs et orbis*, still the ground
Of generation and the roots are sound.
And yet, although the roots are sound enough,

A blight has touched the branches and the fruit.
The voice of wisdom falters and falls off
In aimless speculation and dispute.
The single, sure, tradition and the tough
Old faiths that fed and fostered it are mute,
And Italy, from which the West arose,
Falls prey to new but more barbarian foes.

Italia, O Italia, still in fetters,
Though risen at last, restored, united, free,
I too shall bring you from the world of letters
One more lament, though it is not for me
Perhaps to try to emulate my betters.
The tragic theme, the bough of prophecy
I leave to Dante, Ariosto, Byron
Whose ages range from gold to brass to iron.

But mine's the age of plastics and alloys
Which bring combustion engines in their train
To fill with hideous and inhuman noise
All your once pleasant cities of the plain.
It is the curse of Hell that it destroys
Good of the intellect; the heat, the pain,
The darkness and the terror and the thirst,
Are damnable, but not damnation's worst.

Though Dante found it crowded, hot and smelly,
His first impressions and most lasting were:
Accenti d'ira, orribili favelle,
The sounds of torment, discord and despair,
Screams from the tortured and the brute bass belly
Chuckle of demons; yet if I might dare
Cap Dante I should give for "Hell let loose"
The din Italian motor-bikes produce.

It blinds the heart, it breaks the mind with menace,
Beats, batters, deafens, bruises, numbs, appals,
Ruins Rome's surge of life and blasts Ravenna's
Millennial slumber in her crumbling walls.
And pulverizes every town but Venice
Which, God be praised, is saved by the canals.
Hearing it now it seems to signify
The burden of the poet's anguished cry:

Servi Italia di dolore ostello!
As one by one your tyrants had their hour
The arts could flourish still, and though the fellow
Of lust and greed, the tree of man still flower;
But what can vie with this mechanic bellow,
The final brutal voice of naked power,
As you, who spoke for Europe in your day,
Become its symbol for the mind's decay?

You spoke for Europe as you spoke for Man,
Taught him to pray, to probe, to dream, to dare;
In you his new entelechy began
Where now the yawp of Babel fills the air.
Who speaks for Europe now? The few who can
Know only the recourses of despair;
And none arise to find, renew, prolong
The harmonies of your enchanted song,

A song the Sybil's murmur taught to grow
From age to age, until the centuries
Heard the high trumpets in their passion blow,
Now lost in mindless roar from the abyss.
The parables of history can show
Surely no sadder irony than this
Which brings that noble, intellectual voice
To drown in trivial and distracting noise.

A COMMINATION

He that is filthy let him be filthy still.

REV. 22.11

Like John on Patmos, brooding on the Four
Last Things, I meditate the ruin of friends
Whose loss, Lord, brings this grand new Curse to mind.
Now send me foes worth cursing, or send more
—Since means should be proportionate to ends—
For mine are few and of the piddling kind:

Drivellers, snivellers, writers of bad verse,
Backbiting bitches, snipers from a pew,
Small turds from the great arse of self-esteem;
On such as these I would not waste my curse.
God send me soon the enemy or two
Fit for the wrath of God, of whom I dream:

Some Caliban of Culture, some absurd
Messiah of the Paranoiac State,
Some Educator wallowing in his slime,
Some Prophet of the Uncreating Word
Monsters a man might reasonably hate,
Masters of Progress, Leaders of our Time;

But chiefly the Suborners: Common Tout
And Punk, the Advertiser, him I mean
And his smooth hatchet-man, the Technocrat,
Them let my malediction single out,
These modern Dives with their talking screen
Who lick the sores of Lazarus and grow fat,

Licensed to pimp, solicit and procure
Here in my house, to foul my feast, to bawl
Their wares while I am talking with my friend,
To pour into my ears a public sewer
Of all the Strumpet Muses sell and all
That prostituted science has to vend.

In this great Sodom of a world, which turns
The treasure of the Intellect to dust
And every gift to some perverted use,
What wonder if the human spirit learns
Recourses of despair or of disgust,
Abortion, suicide and self-abuse.

But let me laugh, Lord; let me crack and strain
The belly of this derision till it burst;
For I have seen too much, have lived too long
A citizen of Sodom to refrain,
And in the stye of Science, from the first,
Have watched the pearls of Circe drop on dung.

Let me not curse my children, nor in rage
Mock at the just, the helpless and the poor,
Foot-fast in Sodom's rat-trap; make me bold
To turn on the Despoilers all their age
Invents: damnations never felt before
And hells more horrible than hot and cold.

And, since in Heaven creatures purified,
Rational, free, perfected in their kinds
Contemplate God and see Him face to face,
In Hell, for sure, spirits transmogrified,
Paralysed wills and parasitic minds
Mirror their own corruption and disgrace.

Now let this curse fall on my enemies,
My enemies, Lord, but all mankind's as well,
Prophets and panders of their golden calf;
Let Justice fit them all in their degrees;
Let them, still living, know that state of hell,
And let me see them perish, Lord, and laugh.

Let them be glued to television screens
Till their minds fester and the trash they see
Worm their dry hearts away to crackling shells;
Let ends be so revenged upon their means
That all that once was human grows to be
A flaccid mass of phototropic cells;

Let the dog love his vomit still, the swine
Squelch in the slough; and let their only speech
Be Babel; let the specious lies they bred
Taste on their tongues like intellectual wine;
Let sung commercials surfeit them, till each
Goggles with nausea in his nauseous bed.

And, lest with them I learn to gibber and gloat,
Lead me, for Sodom is my city still,
To seek those hills in which the heart finds ease;
Give Lot his leave; let Noah build his boat,
And me and mine, when each has laughed his fill,
View thy damnation and depart in peace.

LETTER FROM THE LINE

Island-hopping in the rough, the rumbustious season,
The migratory poet, most solitary of birds,
Having left Los Angeles with a *Kyrie eleison*,
Repacks his baggage of carefully chosen words.

For lucky Jim has given his last lecture,
From the bogus mission his wits emerge alive,
From a land where, despite de Tocqueville's shrewd conjecture,
The liberal arts, like living fossils, survive.

Now in mid-Pacific he looks before and after
Astride the equator, surveys each hemisphere;
And his heart on the watershed between tears and laughter
Is glad to be crossing but cross that you are not here.

Glad not to peddle his prestidigitation
Nor to sing for his supper in islands of alien speech;
Though the natives were friendly enough in their own fashion,
Rubbed noses, hung him with flowers, danced for him on the beach;

Glad, though his mirth is a species of comic horror,
To have seen the salaried Muses display their skill
In the universities of Sodom and Gomorrah:
Blind Homer, Blind Harry treading corn at the mill;

To have seen a land whose living tissues function
Better, they say, with a mechanical heart;
Where the surgeon invites the loblolly boy with unction
To open him up and take his organs apart;

Where the supermarket dictates the range of desire
And the passions are packaged: take the largest pack and you save,
But the jumbo-size blonde who is given free to each buyer
May be turned in for cash if that's what you'd rather have.

Glad—but of course such observations are silly:
Travellers' tales are as tall as their comments are snide.
To a visiting comet the cosmos is bound to look chilly
And the whale doesn't look his best when you travel inside.

But now, sweeping back on the outward arc of its passage,
Sadly the comet surveys its luminous tail,
And, nearing Nineveh with his useless message,
Jonah regrets the belly of the whale.

For you, my friends, are still in the monster's belly,
We were warm there for a while, we found it fun
To tickle his ribs inside till he shook like a jelly
And gaped with his gullet to give us a glimpse of the sun.

I may not see you again. As the vessel's motion
Carries me towards my past I review my loss
And the Bear dips down, while glittering from the ocean
Coldly the seven stars dredge up their Cross.

A BLASON

My foundling, my fondling, my frolic first-footer,
My circler, my sidler, shy-sayer yes-and-no,
Live-levin, light-looker, darter and doubter,
Pause of perhaps in my turvey of touch-and-go;

My music, my mandrake, merrythought to my marrow-bone,
Tropic to my true-pole and ripe to my rich,
Wonderer, wanderer, walker-in-wood-alone,
Eye-asker, acher, angel-with-an-itch;

My tittup, my tansy, tease-tuft in tumble-toil,
My frisker, my fettler, trickster and trier,
Knick-knacker, knee-knocker, cleaver in kindle-coil,
My handler, my honeysuckler, phoenix-on-fire;

My cunny, my cracker-jack, my cantrip, my kissing-crust,
Rock-rump and wring-rib in wrestle of randy-bout,
Lithe-lier, limber-leg, column of counter-thrust,
My heave-horn, my hyphener, dew-dealer in-and-out;

My, ah, my rough-rider now; my, oh, my deep-driver,
Burly-bags, bramble-ball, brace-belly, bruise-bud,
Shuttle-cock, slow-shagger, sweet-slugger, swift-swiver,
My, YES now and yes NOW—rip, river and flood!

My breacher, my broacher, my burst-boy, my bubblyjock,
My soberer, slacken-soon, numb-nub and narrower,
My wrinkler, my rumplet, prim-purse of poppycock,
Slither-slot, shrivel-shaft, shrinker and sorrower;

My soft-sigher, snuggle-snake, sleeper and slaker,
My dandler, my deft-dear, dreamer of double-deal,

And, oh, my wry-writher, my worker and waker,
Stirrer and stander now, fledge to my feel;

My prodigy, prodigal, palindrome of pleasure,
Rise-ripe and rive-rose, rod of replevin,
Now furrow my fallow, now trench to my treasure,
Harvester, harbinger, harrow my heaven.

THE COASTS OF CERIGO

Half of the land, conscious of love and grief,
Half of the sea, cold creatures of the foam,
Mermaids still haunt and sing among the coves.
Sailors, who catch them basking on the reef,
Say they make love like women, and that some
Will die if once deserted by their loves.

Off shore, in deeper water, where the swell
Smokes round their crests, the cliffs of coral plunge
Fathom by fathom to the ocean floor.
There, rooted to the ooze-bed, as they tell,
Strange sister to the polyp and the sponge,
To holothurian and madrepore,

The Labra wallows in her bath of time
And, drowned in timeless sleep, displays the full
Grace of a goddess risen from the wave.
Small scarlet-crabs with awkward gestures climb
Through the black seaweed drifting from her skull.
Her ladylegs gape darkly as a cave,

And through the coral clefts a gleam and gloom
Reveal the fronded arch, the pelvic gate;
Spotted and barred, the amorous fish swim in.
But in that hollow, mocking catacomb
Their love-songs echo and reverberate
A senseless clamour and a wordless din.

The love-trap closes on its gullible prey
Despite their sobs, despite their ecstasies.
Brilliant with tropic bands and stripes, they dart
Through a delicious juice which eats away
Their scales and soon dissolves their goggle eyes
And melts the milt-sac and the pulsing heart.

The divers on these coasts have cruel hands;
Their lives are hard; they do not make old bones;
The brutal masters send them down too deep.
But sometimes, as he combs the clefts and sands,
Among the oyster-beds and bearded stones
One comes upon the Labra fast asleep

And throws away his knife, his bag of pearl,
To take her in his arms and wrench her free.
Their bodies cling together as they rise
Spinning and drifting in the ocean swirl.
The seamen haul them in and stand to see
The exquisite, fabled creature as she dies.

But while in air they watch her choke and drown,
Enchanted by her beauty, they forget
The body of their comrade at her side,
From whose crushed lungs the bright blood oozing down
Jewel by ruby jewel from the wet
Deck drops and merges in the turquoise tide.

LAST LOOK

His mind, as he was going out of it,
Looked emptier, shabbier than it used to be:
A secret look to which he had no key,
Something misplaced, something that did not fit.

Windows without their curtains seemed to stare
Inward—but surely once they had looked out.
Someone had moved the furniture about
And changed the photographs: the frames were there,

But idiot faces never seen before
Leered back at him. He knew there should have been
A carpet on the boards, not these obscene
Clusters of toadstools sprouting through the floor.

Yet Arabella's portrait on the wall
Followed him just as usual with its eyes.
Was it reproach or pleading, or surprise,
Or love perhaps, or something of them all?

Watching her lips, he saw them part; could just
Catch the thin sibilance of her concern:
"O Richard, Richard, why would you not learn
I was the only soul that you could trust?"

Carefully, carefully, seeming not to know,
He added this remembrance to his store.
Conscience, in uniform beside the door,
Coughed and remarked that it was time to go.

High time indeed! He heard their tramping feet.
To have stayed even so long, he knew, was rash.

The mob was in the house. He heard the crash
Of furniture hurled down into the street.

"This way!" the warder said. "You must be quick.
You will be safe with us"—He turned to go
And saw too late the gaping void below.
Someone behind him laughed. A brutal kick

Caught him below the shoulders and he fell.
Quite slowly, clutching at the passing air,
He plunged towards the source of his despair
Down the smooth funnel of an endless well.

AN EPISTLE

EDWARD SACKVILLE TO VENETIA DIGBY

Ainsi, bruyante abeille, au retour du matin,
Je vois changer en miel les délices du thym.

First, last and always dearest, closest, best,
  Source of my travail and my rest,
The letter which I shall not send, I write
  To cheer my more than arctic night.
Sole day and all my summer in that year
  Of darkness, you were here,
Were here but yesterday, and still I go
  Rapt in its golden afterglow.
Caught in the webs of memory and desire,
  The cooling and the kindling fire,
Through all this house, from room to room I pace:
  Here at the stair we met; this place

You sat in; still I see you sitting there,
  As though some trace the printless air
Retained; a tremulous hush, as though you spoke,
  Enchants its silence; here your cloak
I held for you and here you looked farewell
  And went, but did not break the spell,
By which I feel you here yet know you gone—
  So men, who winking see the sun
And turn into the dark, awhile descry
  His image on the dazzled eye.
But like a tale I tell it all again
  And gloss it with a scholar's pen,
For so Love, though he harvest all his store,
  Gleans in bare fields to make it more.
Now like the garner ant when frosts begin,
  I have my harvest heaped within:
Abundance for my year to come, a feast
  Still cherished, still increased;
For all it spends from its ripe yesterday
  The heart shall copiously repay:
Words, glances, motions, all that I rehearse
  My joy transfigures, as great verse
From music may have a perfection lent
  More than the poet knew or meant;
And as the cunning craftsman can prolong
  Through cadences and shifts of song,
And make what was by nature beautiful,
  By art more dulcet, keen and full,
So from one day, one meeting, I prepare
  Music to last me out the year.

Yet I cannot recall it as I should;
  Too much surprised by joy I stood,
A child who finds his long expected treat,

Coming, too sudden and too sweet—
Or greedily I gulped it like a beast
And missed the true, the lasting taste.

"Poor beast," I say, "poor beast indeed, who comes
To be content with scraps and crumbs!
Poor heart, poor Lazarus, overjoyed to wait
The scrapings of another's plate!"
For, though I could restore, vivid and strong,
That late, pure, breathless trance of song,
I know myself but a dumb listener, where
I have sung bourdon to her air.

I that was rich, now at the treasury door
May only glimpse that golden store
Piled in fantastic heaps; the jewelled shrine
Worship, not touch, no longer mine;
At most, a starveling Tantalus, must see
The shadow crop upon my tree
Slide through the hand and from my gaping lip
The mocking naiad glide and slip.

Or rather—for in similes of woe
I lose my way—full well I know
The food was real: 'Twas I who could not eat
The spirit's insubstantial meat,
Pleasure of angels, such as flesh and blood
Taste not, though all may take their food.
I, who have held you in my human arms,
Must gaze as if on ghostly charms,
Or on the painting of a mistress dead—
Yet we both breathe and might to bed.
To bed! At the mere thought I feel arise
That rebel in the flesh, who cries:

"It was no picture we saw yesterday,
  But she, in all the living play
Of light on restless body, limbs, hair, breast,
  Eyes, hands—what need to tell the rest?"
What need? But, ah, what sure recourse of joy!
  This nothing can or shall destroy,
Custom deny nor honour stand between,
  Nor your own change of heart demean.
He whose you are, your husband and my friend
  —I do not grudge it, but commend—
Took, when he took you hence, your picture too
  Lest I should keep some part in you.

What should I care, who had my gallery lined,
  Crowded with pictures of the mind?
What care for silk or lute string who possess
  The splendour of your nakedness,
The lily, the jet, the coral and the rose
  Varied in pleasure and repose?
Three years we lived as blessed angels do
  Who to each other show the true
Bareness of spirit and, only when they would
  Travel abroad, wear flesh and blood.
So clothed we met the world: at set of sun,
  Our foolish, needful business done,
Home we would turn, eager to taste at even
  Our native and our naked heaven.
So now by heart each single grace and all
  Their glowing postures I recall.
Absent, you come unbidden; present, you
  Walk naked to my naked view;
Dead, I could resurrect you from your dust;
  So exquisite, individual, just
The bare, bright flesh, I swear my eyes could tell

You by throat, thighs or breast as well,
Or any least part almost, as your face.

Alas, as courtiers out of place
Speak of the court, I boast and dream the rest.
In exile now and dispossessed
I think of how we used, so long ago,
In that tremendous overthrow
Of our first worlds, when first we loved, first knew
No world except these selves, this Two,
How we would laugh to see that Last World pass
For real beyond our Wall of Glass;
And we untouched, untouchable, serene,
Plighted within our magic screen,
Would pity those without, whose curious eyes
Could see, could judge, could recognise,
Know with the mind, but coldly and in part,
Not with the comprehending heart.
This was our game; and, with the growth of love,
We said, these walls of glass remove;
We re-embody those shadows by our joy;
The frontiers of desire deploy
Until our latitudes of grace extend
Round the great globe and bend
Back on themselves, to end where we begin
Love's wars that take the whole world in.
So little states, rich in great men and sound
In arts and virtues, gather ground
And grow to empires mighty in their day.
And we, we said, more blest than they,
Shall not decline as Persian kingdoms do
Or those the Tartar overthrew.
Who lives outside our universal state?
And all within ourselves create.

Will angels fall twice, or the moon breed Turks?
  Or dread we our own works?—
But even while the architects designed
  The finials, their towers were mined.
He, your child-lover, twice reported dead,
  Once false—but all was false—some said
He died at Pont-de-Cé, and some said not
  But on rough alps his bones might rot—
For whom, though your heart grieved, it grieved as for
  Childhood itself that comes no more,
Yet came, and not as ghosts come from the grave,
  But as strong spirits come to save,
And claimed the love we buried long ago.
  I watched it rise and live. I know,
Alas, I know, though I believed it not,
  The spell he casts who breaks the knot;
And this you told me once and bade me learn
  Even before his strange return.

Now it is I outside our Wall. I stand
  And once a year may kiss that hand
Which once with my whole body of man made free—
  O, my twice-lost Eurydice,
Twice must I make my journey down to Hell,
  Twice its grim gods by prayer compel,
And twice, to win you only for a day,
  The spirit's bitter reckoning pay,
Yet for my first default their just decree
  Grants me to hear you now and see,
As deserts know peace, as barren waters calms,
  Only forbidding me your arms.
Why, since my case is hopeless, do I still
  Exacerbate this wrench of will
Against the force of reason, honour, rest

And all that is in manhood best?
Is not this second Orpheus worse than he
Who perished in his misery,
Torn by the drunken women in their chase
Among the echoing hills of Thrace?
To cherish and prolong the state I loathe
Am I not drunk or mad or both?

Not so! These torments mind and heart approve,
And are the sacrifice of love.
The soul sitting apart sees what I do,
Who win powers more than Orpheus knew,
Though he tamed tigers and enchanted trees
And broached the chthonic mysteries.
The gate beyond the gate that I found fast
Has opened to your touch at last.
Nothing is lost for those who pass this door:
They contemplate their world before
And in the carcass of the lion come
Upon the unguessed honeycomb.
There are no words for this new happiness,
But such as fables may express.
Fabling I tell it then as best I can:
That pre-diluvian age of man
Most like had mighty poets, even as ours,
Or grant them nobler themes and powers.
When Nature fashioned giants in the dew
Surely the morning Muses too
Created genius in an ampler mould
To celebrate her Age of Gold.
Yet think, for lack of letters all was lost,
Think Homer's *Iliads* to our cost
Gone like those epics from before the Flood
As, but for Cadmus, sure they would.

Books now preserve for us the boasts of time;
  But what preserved them in the Prime?
Where did they live, those royal poems then,
  But in the hearts and mouths of men,
Men of no special genius, talents, parts,
  Patience their sole gift, all their arts
Memory, the nurse, not mother, of ancient songs;
  No seraph from God's fire with tongs
Took the live coal and laid it on their lips;
  And yet, until their last eclipse,
Age after age, those giant harmonies
  Lodged in such brains, as birds in trees.
The music of the spheres, which no man's wit
  Conceives, once heard, he may transmit:
Love was that music, and by love indeed
  We serve the greater nature's need.
As on the rough back of some stream in flood
  Whose current is by rocks withstood,
We see in all that ruin and rush endure
  A form miraculously pure;
A standing wave through which the waters race
  Yet keeps its crystal shape and place,
So shapes and creatures of eternity
  We form or bear. Though more than we,
Their substance and their being we sustain
  Awhile, though they, not we, remain.
And, still, while we have part in them, we can
  Surpass the single reach of man,
Put on strange powers and vision we knew not of—
  And thus it has been with my love.
Fresh modes of being, unguessed forms of bliss
  Have been, are mine: But more than this,
Our bodies, aching in their blind embrace,
  Once thought they touched the pitch of grace.

Made for that end alone, in their delight,
They thought that single act and rite
Paid nature's debt and heaven's. Even so
There was a thing they could not know:
Nature, who makes each member to one end,
May give it powers which transcend
Its first and fruitful purpose. When she made
The Tongue for taste, who in the shade
Of summer vines, what speechless manlike brute,
Biting sharp rind or sweeter fruit,
Could have conceived the improbable tale, the long
Strange fable of the Speaking Tongue?
So Love, which Nature's craft at first designed
For comfort and increase of kind,
Puts on another nature, grows to be
The language of the mystery;
The heart resolves its chaos then, the soul
Lucidly contemplates the whole
Just order of the random world; and through
That dance she moves, and dances too.

E QUESTO IL NIDO IN CHE LA MIA FENICE?

Were I the palm tree which your love returning
Chose for its roost of fronds and bitter spices,
Gladly would I embrace you with those burning
Branches from which renewed the phoenix rises,
Though from my ashes on the desolate plain
No palm should spring again.

But were I not that palm, and were the peasant
To fell and faggot me for winter fuel,
Still in the seasoned timber would be present
Such passion, such desire for that renewal,
That in my glowing embers he might see
The burning bird and tree.

COUP DE GRÂCE

Just at that moment the Wolf,
Shag jaws and slavering grin,
Steps from the property wood.
O, what a gorge, what a gulf
Opens to gobble her in,
Little Red Riding Hood!

O, what a face full of fangs!
Eyes like saucers at least
Roll to seduce and beguile.
Miss, with her dimples and bangs,
Thinks him a handsome beast;
Flashes the Riding Hood Smile;

Stands her ground like a queen,
Velvet red of the rose
Framing each little milk-tooth,
Pink tongue peeping between.
Then, wider than anyone knows,
Opens her minikin mouth

Swallows up Wolf in a trice;
Tail going down gives a flick,
Caught as she closes her jaws.
Bows, all sugar and spice.
O, what a lady-like trick!
O, what a round of applause!

THE DOUBLE LOOKING GLASS

See how she strips her lily for the sun:
The silk shrieks upward from her wading feet;
Down through the pool her wavering echoes run;
Candour with candour, shade and substance meet.

From where a wet meniscus rings the shin
The crisp air shivers up her glowing thighs,
Swells round a noble haunch and whispers in
The dimple of her belly. . . . Surely eyes

Lurk in the laurels, where each leafy nest
Darts its quick bird-glance through the shifting screen.
. . . . Yawn of the oxter, lift of liquid breast
Splinter their white shafts through our envious green

Where thuds this rage of double double hearts.
. . . . My foolish fear refracts a foolish dream.
Here all things have imagined counterparts:
A dragon-fly dim-darting in the stream

Follows and watches with enormous eyes
His blue narcissus glitter in the air.
The flesh reverberates its own surprise
And startles at the act which makes it bare.

Laced with quick air and vibrant to the light,
Now my whole animal breathes and knows its place
In the great web of being, and its right;
The mind learns ease again, the heart finds grace.

I am as all things living. Man alone
Cowers from his world in clothes and cannot guess
How earth and water, branch and beast and stone
Speak to the naked in their nakedness.

. . . . A silver rising of her arms, that share
Their pure and slender crescent with the pool
Plunders the braided treasure of her hair.
Loosed from their coils uncrowning falls the full

Cascade of tresses whispering down her flanks,
And idly now she wades a step, and stays
To watch the ripples widen to the banks
And lapse in mossy coves and rushy bays.

Look with what bliss of motion now she turns
And seats herself upon a sunny ledge,
Leans back, and drowsing dazzles, basking burns.
Susannah! . . . . what hiss, what rustle in the sedge;

What fierce susurrus shifts from bush to bush?
. . . . Susannah! Susannah, Susannah! . . . . Foolish heart,
It was your own pulse lisping in a hush
So deep, I hear the water-beetle dart

And trace from bank to bank his skein of light,
So still the sibilance of a breaking bud
Speaks to the sense; the hairy bee in flight
Booms a brute chord of danger in my blood.

What danger though? The garden wall is high
And bolted and secure the garden door;
The bee, bold ravisher, will pass me by
And does not seek my honey for his store;

The speckled hawk in heaven, wheeling slow
Searches the tufts of grass for other prey;
Safe in their sunny banks the lilies grow,
Secure from rough hands for another day.

Alert and brisk, even the hurrying ant
Courses these breathing ranges unafraid.
The fig-tree, leaning with its leaves aslant,
Touches me with broad hands of harmless shade.

And if the urgent pulses of the sun
Quicken my own with a voluptuous heat,
They warm me only as they warm the stone
Or the thin liquid paddling round my feet.

My garden holds me like its private dream,
A secret pleasure, guarded and apart.
Now as I lean above the pool I seem
The image of my image in its heart.

In that inverted world a scarlet fish
Drifts through the trees and swims into the sky,
So in the contemplative mind a wish
Drifts through its mirror of eternity.

A mirror for man's images of love
The nakedness of woman is a pool
In which her own desires mount and move,
Alien, solitary, purposeful

Yet in this close were every leaf an eye,
In those green limbs the sap would mount as slow.
One with their life beneath an open sky,
I melt into the trance of time, I flow

Into the languid current of the day.
. . . . The sunlight sliding on a breathing flank
Fades and returns again in tranquil play;
Her eyelids close; she sleeps upon the bank.

Now, now to wreak upon her Promised Land
The vengeance of the dry branch on the bud.
Who shall be first upon her? Who shall stand
To watch the dragon sink its fangs in blood?

Her ripeness taunts the ignominy of age;
Seethes in old loins with hate and lust alike.
Now in the plenitude of shame and rage
The rod of chastisement is reared to strike.

And now to take her drowsing; now to fall
With wild-fire on the cities of the plain;
Susannah! . . . . Yet once more that hoarse faint call,
That rustle from the thicket comes again?

Ah, no! Some menace from the edge of sleep
Imposes its illusion on my ear.
Relax, return, Susannah; Let the deep
Warm tide of noonday bear you; do not fear,

But float once more on that delicious stream.
Suppose some lover watches from the grove;
Suppose, only suppose, those glints, the gleam
Of eyes; the eyes of a young man in love.

Shall I prolong this fancy, now the sense
Impels, the hour invites? Shall I not own
Such thoughts as women find to recompense
Their hidden lives when secret and alone?

Surprise the stranger in the heart, some strong
Young lion of the rocks who found his path
By night, and now he crouches all day long
Beside the pool to see me at my bath.

He would be there, a melancholy shade
Caught in the ambush of his reckless joy,
Afraid to stir for fear I call, afraid
In one unguarded moment to destroy

At once the lover and the thing he loves.
Who should he be? I cannot guess; but such
As desperate hope or lonelier passion moves
To tempt his fate so far, to dare so much;

Who having seen me only by the way,
Or having spoken with me once by chance,
Fills all his nights with longing, and the day
With schemes whose triumph is a casual glance.

Possessed by what he never can possess,
He forms his wild design and ventures all
Only to see me in my nakedness
And lurk and tremble by the garden wall.

He lives but in my dream. I need repel
No dream for I may end it when I please;
And I may dream myself in love as well
As dream my lover in the summer trees,

Suppose myself desired, suppose desire,
Summon that wild enchantment of the mind,
Kindle my fire at his imagined fire,
Pity his love and call him and be kind.

Now think he comes, and I shall lie as still
As limpid waters that reflect their sun,
And let him lie between my breasts and fill
My loins with thunder till the dream be done.

The kisses of my mouth are his; he lies
And feeds among the lilies; his brown knees
Divide the white embraces of my thighs.
Wake not my love nor stir him till he please,

For now his craft has passed the straits and now
Into my shoreless sea he drives alone.
Islands of spice await his happy prow
And fabulous deeps support and bear him on.

He rides the mounting surge, he feels the wide
Horizon draw him onward mile by mile;
The reeling sky, the dark rejoicing tide
Lead him at last to this mysterious isle.

In ancient woods that murmur with the sea,
He finds once more the garden and the pool.
And there a man who is and is not he
Basks on the sunny margin in the full

Noon of another and a timeless sky,
And dreams but never hopes to have his love;
And there the woman who is also I
Watches him from the hollow of the grove;

Till naked from the leaves she steals and bends
Above his sleep and wakes him with her breast
And now the vision begins, the voyage ends,
And the great phoenix blazes in his nest.

. . . . Ah, God of Israel, even though alone,
We take her with a lover, in the flush
Of her desires. SUSANNAH! . . . . I am undone!
What beards, what bald heads burst now from the bush!

DALLA SUA PACE

Fischblut loves singing regardless of the song,
Eighth in the line he waits to take his turn,
Yet hopes his rival will not take too long.
One eye reflects a bed and one an urn;
The torches spit and crackle as they burn.

The rapiers keep the time: tick-tick, tick-tack!
One falls; one flees. Fischblut is left alone.
Gently he turns the corpse upon its back
And finds the hand he holds a fist of stone;
The fiddles falter on a semi-tone.

A patter of papouches on the stair,
Fresh from her ravisher, with her hair in pins,
She swoons. He warbles an enchanting air.
His turn has come, for Fischblut always wins;
Off-stage the Catalogue Aria begins.

PSEUDODOXIA EPIDEMICA

By acupuncture or by moxibustion
The soul repairs its vulnerable sheath;
And beetle paste is love's electuary.
True tales and false alike work by suggestion.
Cure palsy with a poison-ivy wreath
Or squeeze the devil's cherry to vamp an eye.

Our questions choose the answers they think good:
What shape is wine? The shape of any cup.
Since what we fancy serves to keep us human,
To keep love circulating in the blood
Its addicts, when they start to sober up,
Reach out and pour themselves another woman.

Let reason ignore the reasons of the heart,
Pure knowledge is a sow that eats her farrow;
But wisdom's children may hear mermaids sing
In latitudes not found on any chart.
Fledged without feet, to miss the hunter's arrow
The bird of paradise keeps on the wing.

Taken full-strength, truth is a drug that kills.
They say that when he rose, the morning after,
Faith took a tot and felt as right as pie;
But, having accurately checked his bills,
Clairvoyance was found dangling from a rafter,
All the true facts reflected in his eye.

He was my green youth, taught me probe and test;
My ripe years wrote of love: "The search is ended;
Green is the only colour of the leaf;
That golden legend was a dream at best."
Yet, now my autumn comes, the boughs are splendid
Blazing with gold and crimson past belief.

A thousand years pen-white was the tradition.
There was the lake: one only had to look
To see truth's emblem paddling in her snow;
The black one was a joke of the logician.
And yet there was a wild swan in my book
Proved him a liar. But how was he to know?

Cygnus mansuetus may be just a bird.
With you my fabled swan, I give up trying
To disbelieve what science cannot prove.
Let ornithology find our tale absurd:
The cob that sings at last when close to dying
May prove at last my parable of love.

VARIATION ON A THEME BY PAULUS SILENTARIUS

Those whom the mad dog bites, have cause
Though crazed with thirst to spurn the cup:
Mad eyes, mad grin and slavering jaws
As they look in, look up

I might have drowned myself, who knows,
Betrayed and sickened and cast off,
But from the black linn's face there rose
Your faithless mask of love.

Now have I drowned myself in wine
And quite dissolved this heart away
And wait, false love, for that condign
Revenge for which I pray;

When parting from your lover's side
You rise, and on his back he snores,
And naked through the house you glide
And press the well-oiled doors,

Raging with such a thirst as lust
Sated engenders on the flesh
And pour yourself a draught in trust
To quicken lust afresh;

Deep, as oblivion laps the dead,
Cool in its crystal gleams the grape,
And trembling you will bend your head
And your bruised lips will gape;

Then shall you shriek and spill the cup
Cold sweat shall trickle on your skin,
To see my drowned man's face look up,
And meet his mad-dog grin.

CONVERSATION WITH CALLIOPE

Finierat dictos e nobis maxima cantus

The proper way to start a poem
Built on the old high generous plan
Is to invoke the Muse; and, though I'm
Bound to placate the harridan,
She can't expect an epic proem:
The trick's been lost; the best she can
Look for in these degenerate times
Is an *O Thou* to start the rhymes.

"O Thou!"—You see it does sound silly—
"Descend, my Muse!"—and that sounds worse.
"Descend and—" "Don't be Uncle Willy!"
She says, appearing just like nurse,
The antiseptic smile, the chilly:
"Well, Master Alec, writing verse?
I'm sure I've told you times enough
I can't be bothered with your stuff.

"Now that you're fat and over forty,
It's rather odd, you must agree,
My sisters having all proved haughty
Though wooed with assiduity,
You find that after all your *forte*
Was writing epic poetry;
And offer me this slightly battered
Bald rhymester—well, I'm scarcely flattered!"

"I'm very sorry, Miss," I mutter,
"Indeed I beg your pardon, Ma'am!
But though we poets spread the butter,

The Muses must supply the jam.
The flood of things I have to utter
Threatens, you see, to burst the dam,
Without your aid, to whom belong
The lost arts of heroic song.

"You may be right about my figure;
It has perhaps filled out of late.
There's no denying that a wig or
Toupee might enhance my pate.
But while you name with wonted vigour
Defects I grant without debate,
Yet there is one aspersion I
Must categorically deny:

"Your imputation of neglect,
That only in the last resort
With failing powers or prospects wrecked
I turn to pay you tardy court,
This, with concern, I must reject.
At fifteen years, or less, I sought
Your aid, and with that aid began
An epic on the Doom of Man.

"Though I suppose its verse was far
From mastery and blank at best,
Though Browning was the avatar
The style too well made manifest,
While Renan's *Abbesse de Jouarre*
Supplied my scheme, yet all the rest
Was mine: contrivance, persons, tales
Made up in Bathurst, New South Wales.

"I gave it up, as you recall,
Before the end of Canto Two,
But not till I had planned it all,
Nor, though a child, until I knew
My bent and heard the poet's call
That brings his promised land in view.
Though forty years have passed I still
Have not forgotten Pisgah's hill.

"Who that has known it can forget
That first fierce moment of elation
When a young poet feels the jet
And vigour of his inspiration?
Not fame achieved compares, nor yet
Can love's supreme intoxication.
And at that moment you were there
And smiling bent above my chair."

"I own," she answers less irately,
"That once you seemed a likely lad.
But think of all I've suffered lately,
The family troubles that I've had.
A sister can't sit by sedately
And see things going to the bad:
There's poor Miss Clio's lost her wits;
Euterpe cursed with sinking fits;

"Terpsichore reels home each night
As drunk as any fiddler's bitch;
And, since the time has passed you might
Behold the Muse without a stitch,
Turned prude at last and laced too tight
Thalia's caught a nasty itch;
Unhinged by neurasthenic dreams
Melpomene just sits and screams;

"Erato—though, I won't deny it,
She keeps her health and earns her crust—
Has lost her figure, needs a diet
And uplift for a sagging bust,
Spends half her nights in maudlin riot
And works for an Amusement Trust;
Urania's lost the common touch
And only talks in Double Dutch;

"And Polyhymnia's on a pension:
The sacred arts are out of date;
Gods are not asked for intervention
To save a technocratic state;
And if by chance or by intention
She's present when they celebrate,
It is with an embarrassed air
She mumbles some archaic prayer;

"As for myself, I must admit I
Am on the shelf, and that's a fact,
The ramparts of my Trojan city
In ruins and its temples sacked,
And not by poets, more's the pity,
Critics and scholars range the tract
Where Milton sang the world's *Te Deum*,
To pick up bits for their museum.

"For since society has ended
Its ancient pact with the divine,
The public actions which depended
On common faith to make them shine
Once gone, what use is left the splendid
Impetus of the epic line?
The chronicle of prose survives
For the small beer of private lives.

"My sister Clio shares, of course,
At least a measure of the blame;
An epic loses half its force
Not built round some historic name,
Some legend which at least for source
Has deeds that Truth will not disclaim;
Its greatness rests on a conviction
That heroes happen outside fiction.

"And since historical research
Has lost the name of noble action,
Proved most ideas in state and church
Mere subterfuge of greed and faction,
That great men do not lead: they lurch
Between rebellion and reaction,
By documented texts it can
Abolish the Uncommon Man.

"And as for the Uncommon Woman
Who blessed the Hero's hearth and bed,
Divine Calypso or the human
Penelope he chose instead,
Your psychological acumen
Thrusts in where angels fear to tread
And proves her something in between
A mirage and a love-machine."

"Madam," I say, "although no stranger
To the misfortunes you relate,
I can't believe your fame in danger
Or think the mode so out of date;
For though the dog is in the manger,
No hand has locked the stable gate:
The wingèd horse is free and still
May light upon your sacred hill.

"The Muses and the modes you mention
Have fallen, I grant, on evil days;
Slovenly craft and cheap invention
May parch the spring and blast the bays,
Your art alone, without declension
Preserves its splendour and its praise."
"Poor comfort," she retorts, "and small
When no one writes it now at all.

"The epics of the past perhaps
Survive like Tadmor in the waste,
Impressive still, but in the lapse
Of ages men first lose the taste
And then the skill; while, on the maps
Their sites forgotten or misplaced,
They wait, as ancient ruins should,
For Horace Walpole's Mr Wood.

"There was a time the poet's mission
Was to give men their daily bread,
The crown of life, the timeless vision
Which linked the living with the dead.
When Homer spoke, the great tradition
Of verse commanded, taught and led;
With Milton it began to nod,
And Cowley was its *Ichabod*.

" 'Who now reads Cowley?' Who indeed
Reads Homer now or his translator
But schoolboys and the dons who breed
Their kind in every empty crater?
Can some fresh Milton rise to feed
Blind mouths in Learning's incubator,
Or Pegasus his flight renew
Boiled down for academic glue?

"For after Cowley came Defoe's
Invention of domestic fiction;
The comic epic dressed in prose
Drove out heroic deeds and diction;
Pamela's budget of chaste woes
Pleased more than Homer's whole depiction
Of Troy and Milton's War with Hell
Less than the Death of Little Nell.

"So by a sort of Gresham's Law
The novel rose, the epic died,
Nor could be resurrected nor
Remade, for all that Arnold tried.
'What did they kill each other for?'
Old Kaspar's small granddaughter cried,
Which marked, since Kaspar could not say,
How a whole world had passed away.

"Well, if you still would venture on it,
Go in and try it: you will find
To poems longer than a sonnet
Your readers deaf, your critics blind.
Even the few prepared to con it
Will lack enlargement of the mind.
No lion-soul acquires its habit
From close acquaintance with the rabbit.

"Long narratives are out of fashion;
Sustained invention does not please;
And sacred truth and moral passion
Belong to former centuries.
Yet epic stakes its reputation
On public taste for things like these.
Readers who give your poem a glance
Will settle for a police romance."

"All that you urge is cogent, Madam,"
I say, "and sure the Muse knows best;
Yet if a simple son of Adam
May speak and venture to contest,
The epic gifts, suppose I had 'em,
Will quickly put me to the test
And if I fail, I may at least
Make way against the Blatant Beast."

"Well, if you must, you must, my hearty,"
She answers with a little frown.
"If *con amore* match *con arte*,
My scholar yet may grace the gown.
But if we must prolong this party,
You might invite me to sit down,
For legs, though not of mortal clay
Will tire and I have more to say."

"A thousand pardons, pray be seated;
Allow me to pull up a chair!
Forgive me, being somewhat heated,
If I forget the proper care
With which the Muses should be treated:
Their visits are extremely rare.
To honour this poor house of mine,
May I suggest a glass of wine?"

"Thank you, although the drink I treasure
I don't suppose you have—I mean
Of course to ask you for a measure
Of pure, unblushing Hippocrene?
No? Well, I should accept with pleasure
A drop of anything between
From nectar down to mortal pottle;
No glasses though: bring out the bottle!"

The wine poured out, I take my chair.
She tastes and nods and says: "Not bad!
Now let's get back to where we were:
Your epic poem. Suppose you had
The wit, have you the time to spare?
That *jeu d'esprit*, your *Dunciad*,
Cost you six months, as I recall,
And only four books, after all.

"Four books and comic stuff at that,
And yet it caused you quite a coil
Before you had it neat and pat,
Long days of unremitting toil
And nights of labour when you sat
Keeping your modest pot aboil
Or tossed in fever on your bed
With verses seething in your head.

"Can you conceive the dedication
Those mighty works demand? Or can
You summon up the concentration,
That service of the entire man
Required to plan, to mould, to fashion
To grind the grain and bolt the bran?
A task so long, so great, so dread,
So Pope, my foster child, once said,

"As leaves a man, this side the grave,
Scarce time to breathe, no time to be
Friend, neighbour, husband, nay, to have
The care to plant and tend a tree,
Much less in the long run, to save
His soul or meet eternity.
If not, just fold the napkin round
And hide your talent in the ground."

"Ah, there's the rub indeed," I say;
"The doubt you raise, I feel and share it.
Most poets are employed today,
Own cars, eat well, drink vintage claret
—Your glass is empty by the way—
Hogarth's poor poet in his garret
Or truckling at a patron's board
Has gone for ever, praise the Lord!

"But though the Lord be praised, I wonder
Are poets so much better off?
Though now they have their share of plunder
And get both forefeet in the trough,
To earn their bread they have to squander
The hours they once were masters of;
In fact the poet's calling pays
Much worse than in the bad old days.

"Those bad old days (would they were with us!)
Saw Aristo trim his light,
Debase his art, deploy his mythus
To lick the boots of Este's knight.
Well, let it wring the critic's withers,
At least he had the time to write.
Odd jobs as envoy or commando
Still left him years for his *Orlando*.

"Admit he flattered, grant the note
Of adulation gross and crass,
The King of France who turned his coat
Considered Paris worth a mass.
And shall I sneer while I devote
My days to lecture-room and class?
There's nothing sours the Muses' soil
Like eight good hours of honest toil.

"And while that garden blights and sours
On which a full sun rarely shines,
The poets labour after hours
To raise a crop of stunted lines,
Like serfs who round the baron's towers
By day manure the baron's vines
And, while exhausted muscles groan,
By moonlight cultivate their own.

"The serf well knew the serf's condition;
He knew his wine was harsh and thin.
The well-fed poet's dwindling vision
Soon cuts his coat to suit his skin,
Thinks the great tuns of the tradition
Not equal to his kilderkin,
And that no House of Fame surpasses
His week-end cottage on Parnassus.

"See Esau tamed, in Jacob's lobby
Run errands now for Jacob's house;
His birthright bartered for a job, he
Plans mountains that bring forth a mouse;
For art diminished to a hobby
Yields just what hobby-time allows.
Why does he do it? Save your breath:
As poet he would starve to death.

"Take my own case: the world of letters
Is what, God help me, I profess;
For lecturing about my betters
Each year they pay me more or less
Four thousand pounds. Ask what I get as
Poet!—at a random guess
For poems forged with sweat and tears,
Four hundred pounds in forty years!

"Now take the Greeks—" Says she, "Young fellow
I'd rather hear you on the purse.
Your theme grows warm as you grow mellow
(Though frequently your rhymes get worse).
Let's take the Greeks; but please don't bellow.
You argue prettily in verse.
Go on! I like to hear you speak,
Especially as you know no Greek.

"And on the Greeks, you might recall,
The towns which strove for Homer dead
To build him a memorial
Were those where Homer begged his bread.
There never was an age at all
Gave poets three meals and a bed
Though every age is apt to cast
Regretful glances at the past.

"In every Paradise, professor,
The charmer lures, the serpent lurks;
When academic chores depress or
Committees gall and teaching irks,
Just think of Chaucer, the Assessor
Of Customs and the Clerk of Works;
And yet by candlelight he made
The time for *Troilus and Criseyde.*

"Think of Camoens as trustee
Serving the absent and the dead;
Hated, reviled, imprisoned, he
Could still contrive his *Lusiad*;
View Milton in his misery
Unfaltering, and Tasso mad,
And judge if your condition bears
The least comparison with theirs.

"What genius has a mind to speak
Mere circumstance will rarely throttle,
But, if the wine is thin and weak,
It makes no sense to blame the bottle.
Our hidden cause is still to seek;
It is not found in Aristotle
For he was born before the long
Decline and fall of epic song.

"He knew it at its peak and prime
And gave no thought to its decay.
Longinus too, on the sublime,
On this had nothing much to say
And Vida looked to see it climb
To greater triumphs in his day.
But what the worthies never knew
The steadfast Muses keep in view.

"The gift of prophecy they hold,
Although it is the lesser gift,
The past and future they behold
And poets sometimes catch its drift,
Catch glimpses of the Age of Gold
And sometimes see the curtain lift
Upon the face of things to come
When other oracles are dumb.

"But though the Muse bestows the vision
She very seldom gives it scope,
Lest prophecy subvert his mission
By fostering the poet's hope
Through dim surmise and intuition
To cast creation's horoscope:
The task for which we grant the bays
Is still to celebrate and praise.

"That task in which he may not shirk or
Falter, on his hope of bliss,
Die unbegreiflich hohen Werke
(The Devil himself once vouched for this)
Is, nobly, without crank or quirk or
Default, to show it as it is,
And through his art to bring to birth
New modes of being on the earth.

"This is the task that we assign,
Not to haruspicate or scry;
The poet's part in the divine
Stops this side of divinity—
Let's have another flask of wine
Before I start to prophesy,
For now the time has come to show
Things that the Muse alone can know."

I fetch the second bottle out
And while I draw the cork, I ask:
"First would you please resolve a doubt?
If celebration is our task,
I think I know what *that's* about;
The second part still wears the mask.
What does it mean—or must I wait?—
New modes of being to create?"

"Some truths can not be uttered save
By myth," she says, "or like recourses:
(Socrates' Fable of the Cave;
Swift's Fable of the Talking Horses).
Though Wittgenstein turn in his grave,
The mind has other means and forces
'Whereof one cannot speak' to show
The inenarrable we know.

"So, *pace* Wittgenstein, I shall
Tell you my meaning in a fable;
And, though you may not grasp it all,
It has a grace which may enable
The heart to answer to its call;
While Logic built its Tower of Babel
The truth it seeks and seeks in vain
May fall like dew upon the plain.

"In the beginning was the Word
—My myth, you see, is scarcely new—
But though it *was*, it was not heard;
The earth was void and nothing grew
Upon the barren rock; no bird
Flashed singing through the barren blue,
And in the blue and barren deep
There was no life to swim or creep.

"It was as wild a world to see
As e'er returned its Maker thanks:
Mountains in savage majesty
Thrust upward in colossal ranks
And searing ice and scorching scree
Ground slowly down their ragged flanks,
While plains upheaving from their beds
Dried out in desert browns and reds.

"And then the Word began to move,
Itself unmoved, the quickening Will,
By infinitesimals it wove
As in the womb it quickens still.
The endless edifice of love
Felt life's first step upon its sill
And in that primal globule furled
Lay all the orders of the world.

"Orders of being come to birth
Evolving in the cosmic dance.
Each fills and each creates a dearth
Filled by the next in its advance:
Enfolding to transform the earth
First came the mantle of the plants
And with the beasts in their degrees
Made up the living entities.

"The joy to see that green brocade
Bald scarps and shadow lake and rill,
Carpet bare clays with lawn and glade
Is something hard to grasp, until
One sees the dead moon-landscape made
By an abandoned copper mill
(As in Tasmania you have seen)
Breathe, burgeon and resume its green.

"Then gradual in the womb of kind
The second mystery began:
The order of the conscious mind
Perfected in the race of man,
Gave eyes to groping needs and blind
And freed the will to search and plan,
A revolution as profound
As that which clothed the barren ground.

"Civilization when it came,
After long ages in the mould,
Formed the new hearth for a new flame,
Though kindled first in tribes too old
To leave a history or a name,
Or see from magic arts unfold
Within the world of mind the third
Order of being from the Word.

"Freed from those ends which men foresee
And meet with predisposing skill,
The arts themselves propose the free
And unknown ends which they fulfil.
To shape the new entelechy
Of life, the autotelic will
Transfigures and transforms the span
Of all we mean by social man.

"But here I ought to make a pause.
You catch my drift?—So far, so good.
New modes of being, till their laws
Prevail cannot be understood
Beyond the process and the cause;
The end will still be misconstrued
By minds unable to apply
The logic of analogy.

"For instance, scientists agree
In thinking, and they may be right,
There was a time when none could see
Except in shades of black and white.
What must it have been like to be
The first few born with colour-sight,
And how could they explain or find
Words to convince the colour-blind?

"That passion of scarlet, turquoise, gold
In feather, scale or leaf or shell,
Orchid or rose as they unfold
Their delicate, breathless miracle,
How could those drab, grey minds be told
With only grey, drab words to tell,
And lash or straitjacket, no doubt,
For those who dared to brave it out.

"Anger or pity, or derision
Would be the least they could expect
Yet, see, they have imposed their vision
And made their foes a dwindling sect,
Achieved by means of binary fission
What argument could not effect;
So, *verbum sap.*, don't preach or shout—
Just work to bring the thing about.

"But now, my friend, we have to turn
To that deferred, prophetic answer;
You cannot guess, divine or learn
The cause, so hear it while you can, sir,
Why epic cannot yet return.
I promised in an earlier stanza
Footnotes to Malthus and remarks
On certain doctrines of Karl Marx.

"But what I have to tell embraces
Much more than Marx or Malthus guessed.
The future of the human race is
Somewhat precarious at best.
The day when mere survival places
All other values to the test
May not be far away; indeed
Man's deadliest instinct is to breed.

"And breeding as he does unchecked
By Nature, Law or Common Caution,
No cornucopia can expect
To pour forth plenty in proportion,
Nor human skills for long perfect
New means to eke his dwindling portion:
Since self-control is too much bother
They'll end by eating one another.

"My main concern of course is not
This anthropophagous dilemma;
Not last decay but that first spot,
The earthquake's first foreboding tremor.
The final inference is what
Should be implicit in the lemma
And what must bring man to the worst
May well pervert his nature first.

"A plague like locusts, lemmings, lice
Breaks out like fire, typhoon, or flood,
And swiftly as it grows, it dies;
The human plague, less understood
Through slow millennia takes its rise,
At every step, so far so good!
And yet as each divide is crossed,
Some measure of the whole is lost.

"Man wants but little, even so
By little wants he is misled:
'Man wants but little here,' you know,
'Nor wants that little long,' was said
By Edwin just about to throw
Fair Angelina on his bed;
Which lost the girl her pilgrim's permit,
And left him an unlicensed hermit.

"Their vows abandoned with their habits
The 'Law of Measure' set aside
Alas, the phrase is Irving Babbit's,
This precious hermit and his bride
Bred, as you might expect, like rabbits
And had produced before they died,
Counting great-grandchildren as well,
Two hundred from that single cell.

"But death by then was just the stitch in
Time devoutly wished by both.
They'd seen the life their love was rich in
Imperilled by its very growth.
It is not only in a kitchen
Too many cooks can spoil a broth,
And families perish by inflation
Into a tribe, a horde, a nation.

"What Edwin found to be the case
Proves true in history's arena:
Huntress or victim of the chase,
Angelica or Angelina,
Each future mother of the race
So ravishing in her demeanour,
By instinct still, and natural bent, is
Another Sorcerer's Apprentice.

"No hunter of the Age of Fable
Had need to buckle in his belt;
More game than he was ever able
To take ran wild upon the veldt;
Each night with roast he stocked his table,
Then procreated on the pelt.
And that is how, of course, there came
At last to be more men than game.

"No matter: man's invention can
Snatch triumph from his worst mistakes.
Soon cuts of beef and pork began
To take the place of feral steaks,
Next bread, and sifting out the bran
He turned his plain loaf into cakes.
—And as for cake, mankind will do
Their best to eat and have it too.

"It does not work: a time must come
—A fact that man is slow to learn—
Patch, plan, put off, explore and plumb,
You face the point of no return;
The Providential Voice is dumb,
And Wisdom, weeping by her urn,
Proffers in place of Nature's fruits
Synthetic pulps as substitutes.

"Effects of over-population
Converge, no matter where you start;
The economics of inflation
Follows the same curve on the chart
To where *ersatz* provides the ration
Alike for belly, mind or heart.
Then Muses geared for mass production
We make, to save *us* from seduction.

"For though it once made Plato groan,
Deceptions in the cause of grace,
We use at times and freely own.
The singer of the Works and Days
Watching his lambs on Helicon
Learned this and told it in a phrase:
'The Muses speak true things at will,
Though falsehoods lie within their skill.'

"Already these factitious muses
Spread their synthetic wares abroad;
Their sooterkins promote their views as
Members of Trust and Fund and Board;
The Great Society produces
Only the arts it can afford,
Stamped, sterilized and tinned and tested
And standardized and predigested.

"Quite soon, let Observation view,
As systems and their nostrums cramp us,
The world from China to Peru,
The wild from taïgá to pampas,
The last tame bison in the zoo,
The last tame poet on the campus
Is all she'll find, poor Observation,
Of all the former free creation.

"Well, there's your answer! In a word
To look for natural forms from this
Synthetic template is absurd.
The Word itself, their genesis
And goal withdraws and is not heard:
With Man disposing, God in his
Good time can scarce propose, or move
By patient, prescient, procreant love.

"So first the great forms, as I said
A while ago, must disappear.
Epic, like tragedy, is dead;
The doom of all the rest is near,
Just as this wine whose living red
Delights the sense must go, I fear,
For where the vineyard stood, will be
A Coca-Cola factory."

So saying she takes her glass in token
And drains it off and sets it by,
The silence as we sit unbroken
By motion, syllable or sigh,
While in my face she reads unspoken
Sad scrutinies of how and why,
And then at last to my relief
She smiles and intercepts my grief.

"There is no need for you to ask it:
If this is how the arts collapse,
Are all the eggs then in one basket?
Do all the poets then, poor chaps,
Labour in vain? And is the task it
Pleases us to set, perhaps
Mere throwing dust against the wind,
As pointless as it is unkind?"

"Why yes," I answer, "while agreeing
That Sodom's arts prevail of late,
Shall no just man succeed in fleeing,
Leaving salt witness at the gate?
And what of those new modes of being
The Muse assigns us to create?
Can, while her mysteries unfold,
She palter, and blow hot and cold?"

"Look in my eyes," she says, "and read
The answer to that doubt, my friend!"
And in that depthless gaze indeed,
Where all uncertainties have end,
Where lights in endless Light recede
And all the partial visions blend,
Rapt by its Universal theme
I hear her speak, yet seem to dream:

"Although the great Un-culture wins,
Though Sodom's values tip the scales,
Another providence begins,
The Word withdraws but never fails:
As in past ages, dressed in skins
And following the forest trails,
In those vast woods, each little clan
Preserved the entity of Man,

o

"So in this next barbarian age,
Small clans we choose and hold apart,
Some few in whom the heavenly rage
Still blazes and keeps pure the heart;
The human jungle sets the stage
Where these new Levites learn their part:
To guard the coals and keep them fanned
And bear them towards the Promised Land.

"Good-bye my friend, the gift of sleep
I leave you, not my gift of song—
That epic power alone I keep
For one unborn. You waited long
But did not sow and shall not reap.
To you the lower slopes belong,
To him the peaks when time is due.
Now sleep—for I have much to do."

CROSSING THE FRONTIER

Crossing the frontier they were stopped in time,
Told, quite politely, they would have to wait:
Passports in order, nothing to declare,
And surely holding hands was not a crime;
Until they saw how, ranged across the gate,
All their most formidable friends were there.

Wearing his conscience like a crucifix,
Her father, rampant, nursed the Family Shame;
And, armed with their old-fashioned dinner-gong,

His aunt, who even when they both were six,
Had just to glance towards a childish game
To make them feel that they were doing wrong.

And both their mothers, simply weeping floods,
Her head-mistress, his boss, the parish priest,
And the bank manager who cashed their cheques;
The man who sold him his first rubber-goods;
Dog Fido, from whose love-life, shameless beast,
She first observed the basic facts of sex.

They looked as though they had stood there for hours;
For years; perhaps for ever. In the trees
Two furtive birds stopped courting and flew off;
While in the grass beside the road the flowers
Kept up their guilty traffic with the bees.
Nobody stirred. Nobody risked a cough.

Nobody spoke. The minutes ticked away;
The dog scratched idly. Then, as parson bent
And whispered to a guard who hurried in,
The customs-house loudspeakers with a bray
Of raucous and triumphant argument
Broke out the wedding march from *Lohengrin*.

He switched the engine off: "We must turn back."
She heard his voice break, though he had to shout
Against a din that made their senses reel,
And felt his hand, so tense in hers, go slack.
But suddenly she laughed and said: "Get out!
Change seats! Be quick!" and slid behind the wheel.

And drove the car straight at them with a harsh,
Dry crunch that showered both the scraps and chips,

Drove through them; barriers rising let them pass;
Drove through and on and on, with Dad's moustache
Beside her twitching still round waxen lips
And Mother's tears still streaming down the glass.

FAUSTUS

Laying the pen aside, when he had signed,
"I might repent, might yet find grace," he said,
"What could you do?" The Devil shook his head,
"You're not the first, my friend: we know your kind.

"Logic, not justice, in this case prevails:
This bond can't be enforced in any court.
You might prove false as hell, but have you thought
The fraud may damn you, though the promise fails?"

"Suppose I use these powers, as well I may,"
Said Faustus then, "to serve the cause of good!
Should Christ at last redeem me with his blood
You must admit there'd be the devil to pay."

The Devil laughed and conjured from the air
A feast, a fortune and a naked bed.
"Suppose you find these powers use you instead!
But pun your way to heaven, for all I care.

"We could have had your soul without this fuss.
You could have used your wits and saved your breath,
Do what you like, but we at least keep faith.
You cheated God, of course; you won't cheat us."

Faustus unclasped the Book: when that first hour
Struck on his heart, a fragment broke away.
What odds? With four and twenty years to pay
And every wish of man within his power!

He asked to know: before the words were said
Riddles that baffled Kepler all lay bare;
For wealth, an argosy walled in his chair;
For love and there lay Helen in his bed.

Years passed in these enchantments. Yet, in fact
He wondered sometimes at so little done,
So few of all his projects even begun.
He did not note his will, his power to act

Wither, since a mere wish would serve as well,
His reason atrophy from day to day
Unexercised by problems, Love decay
Untried by passion, desire itself grow stale,

Till he, who bought the power to command
The whole world and all wisdom, sank to be
A petty conjurer in a princeling's fee
Juggling with spells he did not understand

And when, at last, his last year came, and shrank
To a bare month and dwindled to an hour,
Faustus sat shuddering in his lamp-lit tower
Telling the time by seconds till time went blank.

Midnight had come: the fiend did not appear;
And still he waited. When the dawn began
Scarce crediting his luck he rose and ran
And reached the street. The Devil met him there.

It was too much. His knees gave way. He fell.
"The bond? . . . My soul?" Quite affable the fiend
Helped him to rise: "Don't fret yourself my friend;
We have your soul already, quite safe, in Hell.

"Hell is more up-to-date than men suppose.
Reorganized on the hire-purchase plan,
We take souls by instalment now and can
Thus save the fuss and bother to foreclose.

"And since our customers prefer, you know,
Amortized interest, at these higher rates,
Most debts are paid in full before their dates.
We took your final payment months ago.

"But, as I say, why fret? You've had your fun.
You're no worse off without a soul you'll find
Than the majority of human kind,
Better adjusted, too, in the long run."

Back in his tower Faustus found all bare.
Nothing was left. He called: the walls were dumb,
Drawing his knife, he stalked from room to room
And in the last he found her, waiting there,

That fabulous Helen his magic art had won.
Riches and power, she was their sum and prize;
Ten thousand years of knowledge were in her eyes
As first he cut her throat and then his own.

MORNING MEDITATION

Every day of my life
I shave the beard from my chin,
Suppress the natural man,
Do my bit in the strife
To keep original sin
As much at bay as I can.

Day after day after day,
I wake and lather and scrape;
Looking myself in the eye
I grin at my image and say:
Look at the hairy ape
Wishing himself goodbye!

Grand-dad, he had a beard,
Randy old son of a gun!
Even when it was white
He, if a wench appeared,
Would roar to get her to run
And catch and cuddle her tight.

Father, too, had a black
Stubble upon his chin;
Every day of his life
With a hollow blade he would hack
At the natural man within—
He did it to pleasure his wife.

She was a handsome jade,
Black, undauntable eyes,
Snug bottom and well-turned calf;
When Father had stropped his blade,

He would reach between her thighs,
Pluck out a hair and laugh.

Then in his sixtieth year,
Seeing the black jowl hoar,
He lathered and gave a groan,
Took himself by the ear,
Picked up the blade once more,
And cut his throat to the bone.

Grandfather took his fun,
Rolled in all manner of hay;
Father could bell the cat
But died of seeing it done;
I keep the beast at bay
With a safety razor, at that!

Having no child or wife,
Sin or superfluous hair,
I live by the Golden Rule.
And every day of my life
I think of that sinful pair
And curse myself for a fool.

ADVICE TO YOUNG LADIES

A.U.C. 334: about this date
For a sexual misdemeanour, which she denied,
The vestal virgin Postumia was tried.
Livy records it among affairs of state.

They let her off: it seems she was perfectly pure;
The charge arose because some thought her talk
Too witty for a young girl, her eyes, her walk
Too lively, her clothes too smart to be demure.

The Pontifex Maximus, summing up the case,
Warned her in future to abstain from jokes,
To wear less modish and more pious frocks.
She left the court reprieved, but in disgrace.

What then? With her the annalist is less
Concerned than what the men achieved that year:
Plots, quarrels, crimes, with oratory to spare!
I see Postumia with her dowdy dress,

Stiff mouth and listless step; I see her strive
To give dull answers. She had to knuckle down.
A vestal virgin who scandalized that town
Had fair trial, then they buried her alive.

Alive, bricked up in suffocating dark,
A ration of bread, a pitcher if she was dry,
Preserved the body they did not wish to die
Until her mind was quenched to the last spark.

How many the black maw has swallowed in its time!
Spirited girls who would not know their place;

Talented girls who found that the disgrace
Of being a woman made genius a crime;

How many others, who would not kiss the rod
Domestic bullying broke or public shame?
Pagan or Christian, it was much the same:
Husbands, St Paul declared, rank next to God.

Livy and Paul, it may be, never knew
That Rome was doomed; each spoke of her with pride.
Tacitus, writing after both had died,
Showed that whole fabric rotten through and through.

Historians spend their lives and lavish ink
Explaining how great commonwealths collapse
From great defects of policy—perhaps
The cause is sometimes simpler than they think.

It may not seem so grave an act to break
Postumia's spirit as Galileo's, to gag
Hypatia as crush Socrates, or drag
Joan as Giordano Bruno to the stake.

Can we be sure? Have more states perished, then,
For having shackled the enquiring mind,
Than those who, in their folly not less blind,
Trusted the servile womb to breed free men?

ODE ON THE DEATH OF PIUS THE TWELFTH

To every season its proper act of joy,
To every age its natural mode of grace,
Each vision its hour, each talent we employ
    Its destined time and place.

I was at Amherst when this great pope died;
The northern year was wearing towards the cold;
The ancient trees were in their autumn pride
    Of russet, flame and gold.

Amherst in Massachusetts in the Fall:
I ranged the college campus to admire
Maple and beech, poplar and ash in all
    Their panoply of fire.

Something that since a child I longed to see,
This miracle of the other hemisphere:
Whole forests in their annual ecstasy
    Waked by the dying year.

Not budding Spring, not Summer's green parade
Clothed in such glory these resplendent trees;
The lilies of the field were not arrayed
    In riches such as these.

Nature evolves their colours as a call,
A lure which serves to fertilize the seed;
How strange then that the splendour of the Fall
    Should serve no natural need

And, having no end in nature, yet can yield
Such exquisite natural pleasure to the eye!
Who could have guessed in summer's green concealed
    The leaf's resolve to die?

Yet from the first spring shoots through all the year,
Masked in the chlorophyll's intenser green,
The feast of crimson was already there,
        These yellows blazed unseen.

Now in the bright October sun the clear
Translucent colours trembled overhead
And as I walked, a voice I chanced to hear
        Announced: The Pope is dead!

A human voice, yet there the place became
Bethel: each bough with pentecost was crowned;
The great trunks rapt in unconsuming flame
        Stood as on holy ground.

I thought of this old man whose life was past,
Who in himself and his great office stood
Against the secular tempest as a vast
        Oak spans the underwood;

Who in the age of Armageddon found
A voice that caused all men to hear it plain,
The blood of Abel crying from the ground
        To stay the hand of Cain;

Who found from that great task small time to spare:
—For him and for mankind the hour was late—
So much to snatch, to save, so much to bear
        That Mary's part must wait,

Until in his last years the change began:
A strange illumination of the heart,
Voices and visions such as mark the man
        Chosen and set apart.

His death, they said, was slow, grotesque and hard,
Yet in that gross decay, until the end
Untroubled in his joy, he saw the Word
    Made spirit and ascend.

Those glorious woods and that triumphant death
Prompted me there to join their mysteries:
This Brother Albert, this great oak of faith,
    Those fire-enchanted trees.

Seven years have passed, and still, at times, I ask
Whether in man, as in those plants, may be
A splendour, which his human virtues mask,
    Not given to us to see?

If to some lives at least there comes a stage
When, all the active man now left behind,
They enter on the treasure of old age,
    This autumn of the mind.

Then, while the heart stands still, beyond desire
The dying animal knows a strange serene:
Emerging in its ecstasy of fire
    The burning soul is seen.

Who sees it? Since old age appears to men
Senility, decrepitude, disease,
What Spirit walks among us, past our ken,
    As we among these trees,

Whose unknown nature, blessed with keener sense
Catches its breath in wonder at the sight
And feels its being flood with that immense
    Epiphany of light?

INDEX OF TITLES